Civil War

George Dewey
ADMIRAL OF THE NAVY

George Dewey
ADMIRAL OF THE NAVY

By *FREDRIKA SHUMWAY SMITH*

Illustrated by Albert Orbaan

RAND McNALLY & COMPANY
Chicago · New York · San Francisco

The events of Admiral George Dewey's
career as related in this book are based
upon careful research. Much hitherto un-
published material of a personal nature
was obtained from George Goodwin Dewey,
the Admiral's only son, who lived in
Chicago for some years prior to his death
in 1963, and from Mrs. Edward Byron Smith,
a cousin of the Admiral.

CONTENTS

ILLUSTRATIONS

Chapter 1
Son of Fighting Men

George Dewey won fame fighting for his country in the Battle of Manila Bay. This does not seem strange, since the story of the fighting Deweys goes well back into the days of Colonial America.

In 1674 Philip, chief of the Pokanoket Indians of Rhode Island, rebelled against the English who were occupying more and more of the Indians' lands and attempting to turn the natives away from their ancient religion to Christianity.

Philip himself was, as his father Massassoit had been before him, friendly toward the English. But he felt strongly that if the loss of land continued, the tribe would eventually die. Yet he never intended that war should come from the differences between the red man and the white. When several of his hot-blooded young warriors killed eight or nine Englishmen in revenge for the execution of one of their tribe for murder, "King Philip," as he was called, is said to have wept. For now he knew that there would be war, a definite break between his people and the English. He knew, too, that it would be a war that he could not possibly win.

And so it was. "King Philip's War" spread throughout the New England Colonies and lasted for two years, continuing even after Philip himself had been killed by a traitor among his own men. Many villages were completely destroyed by the Indians, and there were hundreds of men, women, and children killed on both sides. When it was over, King Philip's people had ceased to exist as a tribe.

Fighting in the front ranks of the English colonists was Sergeant Josiah Dewey, second son of Thomas Dewey, George's first American ancestor. Thomas had come from Kent, England to Dorchester, Massachusetts in 1634.

A century later other Deweys proved their willingness to fight for their country.

The last stars of night were vanishing in the light of dawn on April 19, 1775, when Major Pitcairn of the British marines, at the head of a detachment of British soldiers, approached Lexington, Massachusetts. His purpose was to seize cannon and ammunition which, it had been reported, the colonists had stored there.

But the soldiery were not unexpected. During the night William Dawes and Paul Revere had ridden throughout the countryside warning all able-bodied men to rise to the defense of their liberties. Now, hearing the alarm guns and the drums that called the patriots to arms, Pitcairn ordered his men to load and advance at the double, as the

Minute Men, gathering from all sides, formed in defensive ranks on the Commons.

One of the Minute Men who stood at Lexington was George Dewey's great grandfather William.

Only after a deadly volley from the British muskets had killed seven of the Minute Men and wounded nine others did Parker give the patriots the order to take cover. Then they scattered to take up individual positions behind stone walls, behind trees, behind houses. They were joined by others, and shot at the British with deadly effect as the Redcoats retreated through Concord to Boston, their retreat becoming a flight, and the flight a rout. Thus was the first battle, in what became the War of the American Revolution, won by the American colonists.

Less than a month later, William Dewey's brother, Simeon, and Captain Elijah Dewey marched with Ethan Allen and his Green Mountain Boys to the British-held fort at Ticonderoga and held their firelocks at the ready while Allen thundered at Delaplace, the fort's commander, "Come forth instantly, or I will sacrifice the whole garrison!"

Surprised, the confused Delaplace appeared, undressed, holding his trousers in his hand.

"By what authority?" he asked mildly.

And then that proud answer which has become one of the most famous remarks in history: "In the name of the great Jehovah and the Continental Congress," Allen replied.

Apparently that was a combination which Delaplace did not care to oppose, for he ordered his men to parade without arms. The fort was turned over to the American colonists without the shedding of a drop of blood. And two Deweys took part in that victory, as one had in King Philip's War and another had at Lexington.

Captain Elijah Dewey, who was at Ticonderoga, was a son of Jedadiah, great grandson of Thomas. Jedadiah, a preacher, distinguished himself on a Sunday in September, 1777, when he closed his Bible in the middle of a sermon and led his parishioners in a fight with the Hessians, who had just come to town.

Yes, it is obvious that there was fighting blood in the future Admiral of Manila Bay!

Among George's earliest memories were stories of the American Revolution that were told him by his grandfather Simeon, who was born in 1770, and of the War of 1812, which had taken place only twenty-five years before George's birth—almost a Christmas child—on December 26 at Montpelier, the capital of Vermont, in the heart of the rugged Green Mountains.

How many changes may occur in two generations! Many now living can remember vividly George Dewey and the Battle of Manila Bay that made him famous. Yet it is hard to imagine how different was the world into which he was born in 1837 from that of today.

In December, 1837, the United States of America consisted of only twenty-six states, of which half held slaves and half did not. A month before George's birth a printer and newspaper editor of Alton, Illinois, named Elijah P. Lovejoy, had been killed, and his printing press destroyed, by a mob, because he had denounced slavery. Already the heated disagreements between the slave and the free states, emphasized by the formation in 1833 of the National Anti-Slave Party, and more than five hundred abolitionist societies in the North, were whipping up the feeling that was to develop twenty-four years later into the war in which George Dewey had his first taste of battle.

In 1837 the United States Navy was still almost entirely under sail. To be sure Robert Fulton had built a steamship during the War of 1812 called *The Demologos,* or *Voice of the People.* (Later its name was changed to *Fulton the First.*) *The Demologos* was simply a huge floating battery that could be moved from place to place under its own power, with a double hull and a steam-driven paddle wheel in the center. It was a big ship for its time, 156 feet long, 56 feet wide, and with a depth of 20 feet. It was "armored" by 5 feet of wood above the water line, and equipped with a furnace for heating shot, and pumps for throwing water on the deck of an enemy ship, thus wetting the enemy's powder and ordnance and dampening the spirit of his men.

Unfortunately Fulton died before the ship was finished. Also the war ended before *The Demologos* was ready for battle, and the Navy calmly went on its sail-driven way. Fulton's creation was stationed at the Brooklyn Navy Yard as the receiving ship. There her magazine blew up on the 4th of June, 1829, completely wrecking the vessel.

But meanwhile the value of steam was being demonstrated increasingly in river and lake navigation. Two years after George Dewey's birth, work was begun on two large side-wheeler steamships, one of which, the *Mississippi*, was to link two great names in the Navy—those of Matthew Perry and George Dewey. They were completed in 1842. Both were 229 feet long, with a beam of 40 feet, a draft of 15. The sister ship, the *Missouri*, burned to the water's edge at Gibraltar a year after completion. Of the *Mississippi* and the parts it played in Matthew Perry's and George Dewey's careers, and in the history of the United States, we shall hear later.

In many ways, life in the United States of America still resembled that of Colonial days, though the youthful republic was feeling its strength, expanding, pushing forward to the days of its greatness as a world power, which were still to come. The excitement of the Revolutionary War and the War of 1812, and the freedom gained through them, still filled men's minds and influenced the thinking of the young George Dewey.

When, at 75, he wrote the story of his own life, he told of how he was stirred by his grandfather's Revolutionary War stories and of what an impression a life of Hannibal had made on him. On winter days, he remembered, he used to dash up the snow-covered hills of Montpelier, pretending to be that doughty warrior crossing the Alps. For want of more realistic troops, he often used to induce his young sister to follow him and obey his commands.

He tells, too, in his autobiography, of how excited he always was on the first day the state legislature met each year. It was a gala day in Montpelier, with visitors from many surrounding towns, with gingerbread and sweet cider for sale on the streets. While the adults shopped, gossiped, traded horses, and talked politics, the Montpelier boys would waylay the visiting boys on sidestreets and there were pitched battles—not really because anyone was angry at anyone else, but simply to prove whether the home boys or the visitors were the better fighters.

The stories that are told of George Dewey's early years are typical of a nineteenth-century boyhood. He gave amateur shows in his barn, swam like an otter and established a record for staying under water longer than any of his contemporaries, narrowly escaped serious injury by standing too close to a cannon—relic of the War of 1812—when it was fired on Independence Day, and played enthusiastic hooky from school.

The story of one of his escapades is worth telling, for it illustrates not only the tendency he had in his early years to evade authority, but also other sturdier qualities that played an important part in his adult character.

His schoolmaster at the time was one Z. K. Pangborn, a slight young man, whom the boys, and especially George, thought it would be easy to disobey, for he looked like an ineffective weakling. Actually Pangborn liked George, for he later said of him, "he was one of the boldest and brightest of the younger lads, and above all things loved a fight. He was ever looking for trouble, and while there was nothing you could call bad about him, he resented authority and evinced a sturdy determination not to submit to it unless it suited him."

When George looked for trouble with Z. K. Pangborn, he found it, and something more. It was a fine day in winter, with snow on the ground just right for snowballs. After lunch George climbed to the cupola of the statehouse and began to peg snowballs at passers-by. Pangborn sent one of the boys out to tell George to come back to school. George is reported to have replied, "Tell the teacher to go to the Devil."

Pangborn then came out to give weight to his order, but George meanwhile had gathered a small army of his schoolmates, who pelted the young teacher with snowballs —some from the statehouse roof, some from the bushes on the lawn, and some from the rear. The schoolmaster retreated to the schoolhouse, and there was no more school that day.

The next morning George and his schoolmates came smirking into the room thinking that, having got the best of their teacher, they had nothing further to fear from his authority. As soon as they were seated Pangborn called, "Dewey, come here!" George sauntered to the desk and stood there grinning while the schoolmaster unleashed a blistering lecture which ended with a demand that the boy apologize. George laughed at him, saying something like "Try and make me."

George and his schoolmates pelted the young teacher

It was then that he felt the rawhide whip descend, again and again, with amazing force, raising welts on his back. In agony he dropped, writhing, to the floor. Seven of his schoolmates, who had looked on in astonishment as the thin and weak-looking Pangborn had assaulted their leader, then charged the man. The first was knocked down, and the fight was over.

George Dewey always looked back to that day as a turning point in his life. Being essentially fair-minded, honest, and well meaning, he saw the justice of Pangborn's action, and when, the following year, the schoolteacher moved to another school at Johnson, Vermont, George followed him, for he and the teacher had become friends and George recognized that Pangborn's integrity and authority were qualities that he wanted to emulate.

Years later he told Pangborn, "I shall never cease to be grateful to you. You made a man of me. But for that thrashing you gave me in Montpelier I should probably ere this be in state prison."

In later years Dewey became famous as a strict, but always fair, authoritarian. There is little doubt that Z. K. Pangborn and his rawhide whip were at least partly responsible for this.

George's mother died when the boy was five years old, and his father, Dr. Julius Yemens Dewey, took over the functions of both father and mother, which he seems to have carried out even after his remarriage. (In fact, he remarried twice, for his second wife died also.)

"To my father's influence in my early training," wrote the admiral in his autobiography, "I owe, primarily, all that I have accomplished in the world. From him I inherited a vigorous constitution and an active temperament. He was a great deal more than a successful practising physician. He was one of those natural leaders to whom men turn for unbiased advice. His ideas of right and wrong were very fixed, in keeping with his deep religious scruples."

Though Julius Dewey was a doctor, one who healed the wounds of mankind rather than inflicted them on the battlefield, perhaps the fighting blood of the Deweys stirred in him also, for when George was fourteen the good doctor sent him to the Military Academy at Norwich, Vermont. Many of its students were from the South, where the military spirit seemed stronger than it was in the North, and there were frequent arguments between the Southern and the Northern boys over the question of slavery.

And in the year that George entered Norwich, Harriet Beecher Stowe's *Uncle Tom's Cabin*, with its moving denunciation of slavery, was appearing serially in a contemporary magazine.

Bit by bit the forces that enslaved human beings, and those that were rising against slavery were becoming stronger. Bit by bit the inevitable conflict in which the future Admiral of the Navy was to be tested under fire for the first time was drawing closer.

Chapter 2
Midshipman Dewey

The 1840's and the 1850's, during which seven new states were admitted to the union, were great years in America's expansion, in the history of the United States Navy, and in the life of George Dewey.

There was a good deal of sentimentality and distrust of anything new in the Navy's reluctance to shift from sail to steam. Yet in fairness it must be said that there were sound practical reasons for the objections, too. In the construction of the old sidewheeler, which was the first steam-driven vessel, the large paddle wheel and the main driving shaft were high above the water and so exposed to damage by enemy fire. Also the wheel and driving machinery took up a great deal of room amidships which might otherwise have been used for gun emplacements. And, perhaps most important of all in the view of the oldtimers, they interfered with the customary arrangement of masts and sails! No one in that day would have thought of building a ship without sails even though it had steam power!

Yet experiments with steamships continued. The most important and exciting of all the experimental ships of the

The "Princeton"

day was the *Princeton*, built to the design, and under the supervision, of John Ericsson in 1842 and 1843. In a sense the *Princeton* was the ancestor of every ship of the line in every navy of the world today. She was the first fighting ship to be driven by a screw propeller, the first in which all of the machinery was below the water line out of reach of ordinary shot, and the first to be supplied with fan blowers for the forcing of furnace fires. Further, she carried a gun of Ericsson's design that could pierce four and a half inches of iron.

But alas for the *Princeton*! In February, 1844, she steamed down the Potomac River with a distinguished list of passengers, including President Tyler, his cabinet, and others. A twelve-inch gun—the largest piece of ordnance on any ship in the world at that time—exploded when it was demonstrated, killing the Secretary of State, the Secretary of the Navy, a naval captain, and several others, and wounding a number of passengers.

Nevertheless the *Princeton* set the pace for a revolution in the Navy. In 1846 a congressional committee recommended that thirteen screw-propelled steamers be built for the navy at once. Nothing happened as a result until the following year when the building—not of thirteen but of four—war steamers was authorized. And of these four a board of cautious naval officials, still fearing change, decided that three would have side wheels! Only one would have a screw propeller.

It was not until 1854 that anyone seriously considered bringing the United States Navy up to date, but even then no one was willing to go all the way in acceptance of steam power. Six steam frigates with screw propellers were begun and finished in two years, and considered the best war vessels then owned by any nation. Actually, however, they were full rigged sailing vessels with auxiliary steam power, their engines absurdly small for the size of the ships.

Among other important things that happened in 1854 were two:

Matthew Galbraith Perry, having steamed to Japan in the side-wheel steamer *Mississippi*, returned, leaving behind him a treaty with the Japanese Emperor opening up, for the first time in history, the ports of Shimoda and Hakodate to U.S. trade; and George Dewey entered the nine-year-old United States Naval Academy at Annapolis, Maryland.

The story of the founding of the United States Naval Academy at Annapolis is similar in many ways to that of the transition from sail to steam in the Navy—a story of inertia and opposition, of attempts and setbacks.

In 1823 a proposal to found a naval academy had been defeated in the House of Representatives. In 1824 Secretary of the Navy Samuel L. Southard made a similar proposal to the Congress. In 1825 President John Quincy Adams recommended to Congress legislation to bring about the establishment of such a school. Nothing came of any of these proposals.

In 1826 success was almost achieved. The Maryland House of Delegates adopted this resolution: "Resolved . . . that our senators and representatives in Congress be, and they are hereby, requested to call the attention of their respective houses to the superior advantages which the city of Annapolis and its neighborhood possess as a situation for a naval academy, and that they use their best exertions in favor of the establishment of such an institution."

The resolution was read before the United States Senate on February 7, 1826; President Adams again strongly recommended the establishment of a naval school and a bill was introduced. It passed the Senate, but finally died in an argument between the Senate and the House over a number of amendments added by the latter. John Branch, Levi Woodbury, and Mahlon Dickerson, Secretaries of the Navy under Andrew Jackson, all favored formal naval instruction and under them there were a number of appointments of instructors—but no naval academy. In 1844 there were fourteen "naval professors" at sea: one at Boston, one at Norfolk, three at Philadelphia, and three on special service; also three teachers of foreign languages, one at Boston, one at New York, and one at Norfolk.

The tragic explosion on board the *Princeton* in 1844 had angered the Congress and made it look with disfavor on naval expenditures. Indeed, the general attitude was one of indifference to the need of either a navy or an army at a time when the United States was not at war with anyone.

Yet there were some who felt differently about it. One of them was President James K. Polk who appointed George Bancroft Secretary of the Navy in 1845. On two of the most important issues of the day he was on the side of the Angels, so to speak; he believed in a modern and strong American navy, that could be the equal of any in the world, and he was staunchly on the side of the anti-slavery movement.

Bancroft knew that properly educated and trained men were as important to naval success as modern ships, and wanted to establish an academy that would do for the Navy what West Point had done for the Army. But old-time salts, leaders in the Navy, were opposed to it, and Congress would not approve of his idea or authorize expenditures for it. That did not bother George Bancroft. He saw that actually, without any further legislation, it was possible for him to centralize the naval education already authorized and being carried on at sea, at Boston, at Philadelphia, and at Norfolk, and, presto! there would be a naval academy.

Knowing, from the Maryland resolution, that his idea would find a welcome at Annapolis, he made a trip of inspection to the old Army Fort Severn, established on ten acres of ground between the Severn River and Chesapeake Bay in 1808, and now abandoned. There were eight buildings: the fort, the commandant's quarters, a block of officers' quarters, the quartermaster's office, the hospital, quarters for enlisted unmarried men, quarters for married men, and the bakery. With a little cleaning up, and a few adjustments here and there, they would do admirably for a start. And George Bancroft had enough faith in his idea to believe that once his naval academy got under way the results would so fully justify it that money would be forthcoming with which to improve it.

He had no difficulty in "borrowing" the old fort from the Army. In October, 1845, the United States Naval Academy opened its doors, with Commander Franklin Buchanan as its first superintendent. To be sure, only three students reported for instruction that first fall. Nevertheless a great institution had been established. "We owe the efficiency of the personnel of our navy to Annapolis," wrote Admiral Dewey in 1912, "and we owe Annapolis to George Bancroft."

It was rather by chance that George went to Annapolis nine years later. He had wanted to go to West Point. However there was no vacancy in the U.S. Military Academy available to an applicant from Vermont. Had there been, as he wrote later in his autobiography, he "might have gone into Manila Bay on an army transport instead of on the *Olympia*" as commander of the Pacific fleet. Appointments to both the military and naval academies at that time were dependent upon the recommendation of representatives in Congress or senators rather than on competitive examinations, though entrance examinations were required. A Montpelier boy named George Spaulding had received the appointment as a candidate for Annapolis, but at the last moment decided that he wanted to be a minister of the gospel instead of a naval officer. As soon as Dr. Dewey learned that young Spaulding had changed plans, he asked his friend Senator Foote to recommend George Dewey. The Senator did so, and George, not yet quite seventeen, set off for Annapolis with his father.

Today it is not much of a trip from Montpelier, Vermont, to Annapolis. Any good driver with a good car would not hesitate to make a date for supper in Annapolis and leave Montpelier early in the morning in order to keep it. But in 1854 it was no small journey. George and his father went by rail to New York, where they spent the night, after Dr. Dewey had given George enough excitement to last him for months by taking him to the theater. From New York, they took a steamer to Perth

At left: Sketch of Dewey's father; below: Entrance to U.S. Naval Academy as it was in Dewey's day

Amboy, and George had his first taste of the sea which later was to be a second home to him. From Perth Amboy they continued by train, with horses drawing the car in which they rode through the streets of Philadelphia and Baltimore, and a brakeman blowing a horn to warn people to get out of the way of the express! The trip from New York to Annapolis, which now takes something like four hours, took George and his father twelve.

The entrance examinations were fairly simple, consisting chiefly of the three R's—reading, 'riting, and 'rithmetic—and George passed them without difficulty.

Before Dr. Dewey left to return to Montpelier he

said to his son, "George, I've done all I can for you. The rest you must do for yourself."

The words apparently made a deep impression on the boy for he mentioned them more than once in his autobiography written many years later, and is reported to have cried out in delirium on his deathbed, "I hope, Father, you think I have done well."

George had never been a particularly good student, and he took his old habits of negligence and mischief-making into Annapolis with him. But the discipline and importance given to scholarship at the Naval Academy were far more exacting than anything he had experienced before, and his first year there turned out to be almost his last. There were sixty boys in his class when he entered the Academy in the fall of 1854. At the end of the year only thirty-five were left. The rest had been dropped, because of poor scholarship, or misbehavior, or both. Of the thirty-five who remained, George was number 33, with 113 demerit marks. Two hundred marks meant automatic dismissal. He was poor in history and geography but excellent in mathematics, which helped to pull him through.

Finding himself so close to the bottom of the class and potentially so near dismissal must have sobered George somewhat and made him think of his father's final admonition, for he did better in his second year, during which nine more of his classmates were dropped, leaving twenty-six. Of these George was ninth.

Life at Annapolis in George Dewey's day was a rugged, hard-working existence. There were no athletics;

the day of the Army-Navy football game was still to come. The only planned exercise was the regular military drill. Excess energy and high spirits found expression in pranks and fist fights, and "Shang" Dewey (for this was George's Annapolis nickname—he never could remember why) took his part in the ruckusses. These involved not only midshipmen but sometimes instructors as well. At one time an assistant professor whom the boys called "the bullpup" was locked up by the students in a wall cabinet in the chemical laboratory as an expression of student disapproval.

There were frequent fist fights, which were officially discouraged, but actually accepted by the instructors as a part of the boys' toughening up process. A fight that George had, and its consequences, were typical of the way the school looked at it.

A classmate who sat opposite him at mess called him a name which, under youth's code of honor at the time, made a fight obligatory. Without waiting for a more appropriate time and place George went for the other fellow and beat him down under the table. Both were taken to the Superintendent, Captain L. M. Goldsborough (who became a rear admiral during the Civil War) for a serious infraction of discipline. Captain Goldsborough asked George why he had attacked his messmate. When George repeated the name the other had called him, Captain Goldsborough told him that he could not have done anything else, fined him ten demerits, and told the other fellow he had got exactly what he deserved.

At another time he is said to have received and accepted a challenge to a duel, but upper classmen interfered and it did not take place.

This is what life was like for Annapolis cadets at the middle of the nineteenth century. Another reflection of the somewhat rough and ready atmosphere of the day is in the furlough song, which the boys sang in celebration the night before their departure on their first furlough at the end of two years in school.

They must have made a picturesque sight, all dressed alike, in the uniform for acting midshipmen which the book of regulations of the time describes as "a jacket of dark blue cloth, double breasted with side-pockets, rolling collar, nine small navy buttons on each breast, and a gold foul-anchor [that is, an anchor with a length of cable loosely wound about its shank] on each side of the collar. Cap, same as that prescribed for a midshipman, except the gold lace band, instead of which a silver four-anchor over visor is to be worn."

Those who could raise them wore whiskers, and their hair was allowed to grow long, curling out from under the caps and about their ears.

There were, of course, no girls at their pre-furlough gatherings, but if there had been they would have added a touch of what now seems to us to be the long ago, for they would have worn hoopskirts, which were the country-wide fashion at the time.

And this is the song that the boys sang:

Come all ye gallant middies
Who are going on furlough;
We'll sing the song of liberty;
We're going for to go.

Take your tobacco lively
And pass the plug around;
We'll have a jolly time tonight
Before we're homeward bound.

Our sweethearts waiting for us,
With eyes brimfull of tears,
Will welcome us back home again
From an absence of two years.

Tobacco chewing was an almost universal habit for American men in those days and the boys at Annapolis, probably feeling that it proved they were grown up, practised it, George Dewey among them.

Finally the four years at Annapolis passed. Of the sixty who had entered the Academy in George's class, fifteen were graduated. All the rest had dropped out. Of the fifteen, George, who had been almost at the bottom of his class at the end of his first year, stood fifth. Obviously the young man, now twenty years old, was growing up, accepting responsibility, developing those characteristics that he was to show so clearly in his adult life.

Meanwhile other things had been happening that were of vital importance in the history of the United States and had a direct bearing on the life story of George Dewey.

In 1854, the year George had entered Annapolis, the Republican Party had been formed and immediately took part in the most hotly argued issue of the day by opposing the Kansas-Nebraska Act which left the issue of slavery in those two states to be decided by the settlers. In 1856 the party nominated its first candidate for President of the United States, John C. Frémont, who was defeated by James Buchanan. One of the men who campaigned eloquently on behalf of Frémont was a raw-boned lawyer from Springfield, Illinois, who made over fifty speeches for the candidate, and was, in fact, to follow Buchanan as president. His name was Abraham Lincoln.

In that same year the abolitionist John Brown and several of his followers fought pro-slavery forces at Osawatomie, Kansas. Three years later, in what was intended to be the beginning of an action to free all the slaves, he and twenty-one followers seized the U.S. Armory at Harpers Ferry, Virginia. The Armory was retaken by United States Marines led by Lieutenant-Colonel Robert E. Lee, who later became commander in chief of the armies of the Confederate States during the Civil War, and Brown was executed.

But he was not forgotten by those who hated slavery. During the Civil War the soldiers of the North sang, to the tune of the "Battle Hymn of the Republic,"

> *John Brown's body lies a moldering in its grave,*
> *John Brown's body lies a moldering in its grave,*
> *John Brown's body lies a moldering in its grave,*
> *But his soul goes marching on.*

North and South, throughout the United States, the issue of slavery was argued with increasing heat and bitterness. It was emphasized in 1856 and 1857 by the argument of the Dred Scott case before the United States Supreme Court. Dred Scott was a Negro who had been a slave, but had lived for several years with his master in free states. On returning to slave territory he was denied his freedom and attempted to gain it by legal means. The final verdict of the Supreme Court was that a Negro whose ancestors were sold as slaves was not entitled to the rights of a citizen of the United States and that he had, in fact, no standing whatever in court. This was almost like saying that a Negro slave was not a human being, and further inflamed the feelings of the abolitionists. Day by day, and month by month, the great and bitter conflict, in which George Dewey was to play a part, was drawing closer.

Chapter 3
"Join the Navy and See the World"

But these things did not depress young George Dewey, now not quite twenty-one, and a midshipman. He was looking forward to two years' cruising in foreign waters before getting his commission. He was about to see the world, and, by a special stroke of good luck, he, with three other midshipmen, was to be aboard the *Wabash*, flagship of the Mediterranean squadron, the pride of America, and a ship that proved beyond doubt that the United States Navy was awakening from its long sleep and becoming a power to be reckoned with in international affairs.

The *Wabash*, a steam frigate of over four thousand tons, with her batteries arranged at portholes the entire length of her gun deck, was one of six that had been built three years before, in 1855. She was a sister ship of the famous ironclad *Merrimac*, which fell into Confederate hands and was rechristened the *Virginia* during the Civil War. In 1857 the building of five large screw sloops was ordered, and now, in 1858, seven more smaller screw sloops were begun. One of these, the *Pawnee*, was the first vessel with twin screws in the United States Navy. Year by year, vessel by vessel, our Navy was growing up.

Yet the old love for sail and the prejudice against steam still hounded naval design. If, on a picture of the *Wabash*, you were to lay a bit of paper over the single small stack that rises amidships, you would think you were looking at the picture of an old-time sailing frigate, full rigged, with her three towering masts and her bowsprit, and her sails billowing handsomely in the wind. Indeed that is essentially what she was—a sailing ship with steam auxiliary power.

Her maximum speed under steam was nine knots (that is, nine nautical, or about ten and a half land, miles an hour) and her average about five. But when Flag Officer LaValette, a veteran of the Battle of Lake Champlain in the War of 1812, and a lover of sail, would order her two horizontal engines stopped and put her under full sail with a fine wind, she would scud along with the grace and beauty of a sea bird. Then the grand old seaman would walk the quarterdeck with his head high and a joyous lift in his step. The vibration of her two horizontal engines was unnatural! Every steamship stank of the land! The combination of a fine wind and sail was what the good Lord had intended for moving seafaring vessels!

The *Wabash* sailed, or, if you like, steamed, from Hampton Roads on July 22, 1858, beginning a cruise that George Dewey was to remember the rest of his life as one of his finest experiences. The sea voyage from New York to Perth Amboy, which had seemed so exciting to him four years before, now seemed like a little ferry trip, and the boat on which he and his father traveled a toy compared with this, a sea voyage to the Mediterranean, on the finest ship of the U.S. Navy.

Two days out the *Wabash* raised her colors to a Spanish bark, and a few days after that, to the English brig *Fawn,* and George had his first lesson in international courtesy on the high seas. He learned, too, that the voyage to the Mediterranean was not only to give him and his three schoolmates experience at sea, but also played a part in international statesmanship.

Ever since the campaigns against the pirates of the

The "Wabash"

Barbary States, called the Tripolitan War (1801–5), the United States had dispatched a squadron to the Mediterranean once a year. The cruise had several purposes. It showed any ambitious sea ruffian, aspiring to a bit of piracy, that we were as able to put them down as we had been before. It gave us the opportunity to take our place beside the European navies which also gathered there once a year. And joining in the elaborate social functions, which took place both at the Mediterranean courts and on shipboard, kept us in touch with European affairs.

Obviously, then, the next two years were going to be somewhat different from the four that had just passed at Annapolis, when it often seemed to George that school was all work and no play. To be sure there was work to be done on shipboard, as he learned the duties of the deck officer's watch. But it was quite apparent that there was going to be play, too, and excitement, and glamour such as he had dreamed of when he had pretended, in Montpelier, that he was Hannibal crossing the Alps.

On August 15 the *Wabash* entered the Strait of Gibraltar, between the Pillars of Hercules, where George gazed in wonder at the great rock standing guard over the world's largest inland sea. For the next fourteen months, from Gibraltar to Turkey and Egypt, until the *Wabash* was to turn westward once more, he was to witness a round of formal international receptions, balls, and dinners. They were friendly affairs, but in at least one instance he saw an exhibit of something less than friendliness, and, strangely enough, from the English who, in spite of the wars of 1776 and 1812, were traditionally close friends to the United States.

Into the Bosporus, that sixteen-mile-long strait between the Mediterranean and the Black Sea, which was straddled by the ancient city of Byzantium (called Constantinople in 1858, and Istanbul now), the *Wabash* steamed. There she joined the vessels of European squadrons gathered to celebrate the birthday of Mohammed.

This was all very well, but an international agreement had set a maximum tonnage for warships which entered the Bosporus, dictated by jealousy between the great European powers and the fear that one would get the better of another. The *Wabash*, largest and finest of the ships assembled there, had a tonnage in excess of that maximum, and Lord Stratford de Redcliffe, the British ambassador, sent a curt message to Flag Officer LaValette that the *Wabash* must leave. Because of Britain's preponderant influence in the East, he was accustomed to making suggestions to the Sultan which had almost the force of orders.

No one on the *Wabash*, or for that matter in Washington, had any very great interest in the jealousies and intrigues that created ill feeling among the European powers, and LaValette, with a shrug of his shoulders, began to get ready to turn westward. But Mr. Williams, the able United States Minister to Turkey, who had become a little annoyed at de Redcliffe's assumption of authority, felt differently about it, and George Dewey was convinced that what followed came about through his intervention with the Sultan.

While the *Wabash* was being readied to leave, Flag Officer LaValette visited the mosque on the day when the Sultan Abdul Mejiid was to make his weekly visit, and took George along as his aide. The young midshipman was never to forget the brilliant pageant that marked the Sultan's progress to the mosque, between banks of soldiers, surrounded by his brilliantly uniformed staff, and followed by ladies of his harem.

It was always a formal occasion, and filled with deep religious meaning for Mohammedans, but as the ruler left the mosque he did a most unusual thing. Leaving his guard, he walked over to the group of American naval officers, who, with officers from other ships, were watching the ceremonious procession, and came directly to Captain LaValette. While George stood at rigid attention beside his officer, his heart beating rapidly in excitement, the Sultan spoke to the captain. He said that he had heard, to his regret, that the *Wabash* was planning to leave, and asked, as a favor to him, that it remain a bit longer. Otherwise he would not have the opportunity to come aboard the beautiful ship of which he had heard so much.

That changed all plans for the *Wabash*, of course, since she was in Turkish waters and the Sultan was the ruler of Turkey. Perhaps Abdul Mejiid was granting a favor to Mr. Williams, who was well liked in his court; perhaps he was enjoying giving the British Ambassador

George Dewey as a young man; also a replica of his signature

his come-uppance. In any case no further objection was forthcoming from de Redcliffe, and the honors were with the Sultan and the *Wabash*.

Never had the good ship, which was always kept in apple-pie order, been given such a scrubbing and neating up as for the Sultan's visit. The Turkish flag was flown, of course, and every officer and man on board was dressed as though he had just stepped out of a bandbox. Aboard also that day was the American minister, Mr. Williams, and his very attractive daughters. One of them, Mary, brought her autograph book along and asked several of the officers to sign it. She was to stay in George's memory for the rest of his life, and perhaps it was because of her, as much as because he noticed that the officers of the

British and other European vessels did not chew tobacco, that he decided the habit he had contracted at Annapolis was an unpleasant one, and dropped it.

It was not until nearly forty years later that George Dewey, then Admiral of the Fleet, was to see Mary Williams again.

In spite of Lord Stratford de Redcliffe's unfriendly gesture, Dewey was to remember the pleasant relations that existed between the personnel aboard the *Wabash* and the members of the British Navy in the Mediterranean. There were visits back and forth between the ships of the two nations, and they were always like family get-togethers. When the 28th Regiment of British Infantry left the Bosporus on *H. M. S. Perseverance*, everyone aboard the *Wabash* lined the rail and cheered the troops, and when the *Wabash* left the Bay of Naples the ship's band played the British national anthem in honor of the British ships at anchor there, and a British band answered with "The Star Spangled Banner."

Interestingly enough it was at just about this time that an incident, which has gone down in the memory of the Navy as the "blood is thicker than water episode," took place, in which an American ship was of service to the British. Thirty-nine years later, as we shall see, the British Navy expressed its appreciation by giving similar help to George Dewey's squadron in Manila Bay.

In June, 1859, a number of British, French, and American warships were gathered at the mouth of the Peiho River in northern China, carrying ministers of their respective countries to Peking, the Americans under command of Flag Officer Josiah Tattnall.

The Chinese, hostile to all three of the nations whose ships were gathered there, had placed barriers across the river, and given notice that they would fire on any vessel that attempted to pass them. When French and English vessels tried to force the barrier, the Chinese, as good as their word, poured a deadly fire into them from seven forts on both sides of the river. Several of the ships were sunk and there was a serious loss of men. For some time Tattnall watched in impatient neutrality. Then, turning to a ship's officer who stood beside him, he said, "Blood is thicker than water," and got his ship underway, towing barges, on which were several hundred men of the British Navy, up to the scene of action.

Meanwhile word came to him that the British Admiral Hope, aboard his flagship, the *Cormorant*, had been wounded, so he boarded the *Cormorant*, which was then engaged and under fire, to express his sympathy. As Tattnall's boat was a few feet from the British vessel, a shot struck the American ship, killing the coxswain, wounding the flag lieutenant, and so damaging the vessel that Tattnall and his men barely had time to get aboard the *Cormorant* before their own ship sank.

Aboard the *Cormorant* all was action. All of the members of the bowgun crew had been disabled, and while the American officers were paying their compliments to the officers of the *Cormorant*, American seamen quietly went to the bowgun, and joined the fight.

When Tattnall later pointed out to them that they had violated neutrality, one of them said, "Beg pardon, sir, but seein' them so shorthanded we just thought we'd give them a lift for fellowship's sake."

So, in spite of the Revolutionary War, the War of 1812, and the freedom, which both the English and the Americans feel, to criticize each other, so it was and so it has always been between Great Britain and the United States of America. We may have our family quarrels, but when another nation opposes either of us, both of us face it as a common enemy.

Before the Mediterranean cruise of the *Wabash* was over, George had seen Beirut, Alexandria, and, after an overland trip, Jerusalem. On the way out of the Mediterranean the ship visited several Italian ports, and on November 13, 1859, again passed between the Pillars of Hercules at Gibraltar, but this time headed west, arriving at the Brooklyn Navy Yard on December 16.

Truly young George Dewey was proving the truth of what later was to become a Navy enlistment slogan, "Join the Navy and see the world."

After three months' leave of absence, which he spent at his home in Montpelier, George was assigned to the *Pawnee*, the twin-screw sloop begun in 1857, for a cruise to Caribbean and gulf ports. The captain of the *Pawnee* was Henry J. Harstene of South Carolina, a staunchly patriotic southern and pro-slavery man.

At a banquet in Vera Cruz, George heard Captain Harstene say that if South Carolina seceded from the

The Dewey home in Montpelier, Vermont

United States he would take the *Pawnee* into Charleston Harbor and turn her over to the state.

On the return voyage George happened to be officer of the deck as the ship came opposite Charleston. Suddenly Captain Harstene appeared on deck, looking wild-eyed, as Admiral Dewey later reported, and wearing a crazy-quilt blouse made from remnants of his wife's silk dresses.

"Take in the top-gallant sails," he commanded.

George Dewey had them taken in.

"Now set them again," the captain ordered, and Dewey saw that the order was obeyed.

"Now call all hands and take them in properly," the wild-eyed captain bellowed.

Although George Dewey knew that the sails had been managed properly, he made no comment, but called all hands on deck and again ordered the top-gallant sails taken in. He noticed Lieutenant Marcy, the executive officer, and son of a former secretary of state, who had heard Captain Harstene's remark at Vera Cruz, watching his superior officer closely, and saw the look of confused embarrassment that spread over the captain's face as the ship continued on her course.

There was never any explanation of the incident, but Dewey was always convinced that when Captain Harstene had originally ordered the top-gallant sails taken in he had intended to take the ship into Charleston, but that standing before the whole crew, and with Lieutenant Marcy's eyes on him, he found that he could not bring himself to give the order.

In January, 1861, George Dewey returned to Annapolis and took his final examinations, standing third among the fifteen in his class. And so, he reported later, "as I had finished my first year as thirty-third, I was able to report to my father that I had continually improved; and I might say, in view of his warning at the time of my appointment, that I had done 'the rest' reasonably well." In April he was commissioned a lieutenant, at the age of twenty-three.

Chapter 4
South Against North

In 1860, Abraham Lincoln, candidate of the young Republican Party, was elected to the presidency of the United States. He was not an abolitionist, but had made it quite clear that he favored the prohibition of slavery in all states newly admitted to the union, and the eventual end of slavery throughout the United States. This was in line with the basic policy of the "Free Soil Party," formed in 1848 with the purpose of keeping slavery out of the territories acquired from Mexico, a political group that had been absorbed by the Republican Party when it was formed in 1854.

Because of his stand on slavery, the tall, gangling figure of Lincoln, with his stove-pipe hat accentuating the length of his scrawny chicken-like neck, and with the sadness of the world seemingly reflected in his eyes, became a symbol of tyranny and evil to the southern slave holders. There were riotous demonstrations against the "black Republicans" in the South, and a frenzied demand for secession.

The first state to respond to it was South Carolina,

which seceded on December 20, 1860. It was followed by Alabama, Georgia, Louisiana, Mississippi, Texas, Arkansas, North Carolina, Tennessee, and much of Virginia. The western counties of the latter commonwealth, however, refused to leave the Union and formed a separate state called "West Virginia," which, of course, remains separate to this day.

Yet still the issue of war or peace was undecided. There were those in the North who were in favor of saying to the southern states, "Go in peace." But on March 4, in his inaugural address, Lincoln made his own attitude quite clear. Speaking to the South, he said,

"In your hands and not in mine is the momentous issue of the civil war . . . I hold that in contemplation of universal law and the Constitution, the union of these states is perpetual . . . No state, upon its own mere action, can lawfully get out of the Union. I shall take care . . . that the laws of the Union be faithfully executed in all of the states."

From the point of view of the South this was adding insult to injury. Not only was the Yankee president against slavery, but he denied others the right of free men to decide whether they wanted to belong to one association of states or another of their own choosing.

The situation seemed intolerable to the die-hard secessionists of the South. On April 12, five weeks after Lincoln's inauguration, and eight days before George Dewey received his commission as lieutenant, General P. G. T. Beauregard of Louisiana, a graduate of West Point who had resigned his commission to join the Confederate

Army, fired on Fort Sumter in the harbor of Charleston, South Carolina, and two days later accepted its surrender. The Civil War, or (as the South still calls it) the War Between the States, which was to last four years, and in which half a million Americans were to lose their lives, had begun.

Does it matter now, a hundred years later, how many of these half million dead were Northerners and how many Southerners? All were Americans, all had hoped to work together in the building of a great free nation made of a union of sovereign states. Now one group was at the throats of the other in one of the saddest of all sad wars that have split the brotherhood of man.

What was the state of this disrupted union as the war broke upon it? In 1860 the population of the entire United States, North and South, was about thirty-one and a half million, of which about two-thirds were in the northern states. The entire United States Army consisted of about sixteen thousand officers and enlisted men, including a goodly number of southerners—many of whom, on the outbreak of war, left the Army of the United States and entered that of the Confederacy. The Navy consisted of some ninety ships, a third of which were unseaworthy and most of the rest of which were scattered in ports abroad. Some were off the coast of Africa, some in the Far East, and some in South American waters. The secession of Virginia had meant the loss of the great Norfolk Navy Yard, and with it the steam frigate *Merrimac*, which was in the yard for repairs. Rebuilding it as an ironclad, and rechristening it *Virginia*, the South stimulated the North to build ironclads also. The indecisive battle some time later between the southern *Virginia* (the old *Merrimac*) and the northern *Monitor* was one of the most famous results.

Now Lincoln called for 75,000 volunteers—almost five times as many as the total number in the Army before the war—and asked one of the most distinguished generals of the Army, and a former superintendent of West Point, Robert E. Lee of Virginia, to take command of the Army of the North, which, in Lincoln's terminology, was still the Army of the United States of America.

But Lee declined, saying that while he was opposed to secession and civil war, he could not take part in the military invasion of his homeland. Resigning his commission, he went home, became first commander of the Army of Northern Virginia, and later of the entire Confederate Army.

Many officers, in both the Army and the Navy, faced the same conflict as did Robert E. Lee. Captain Franklin Buchanan, the first superintendent of the United States Naval Academy at Annapolis was in command of the *Merrimac* (or *Virginia* as the South called her) during the famous battle between this ship and the *Monitor*. Buchanan, born in Baltimore, was commandant of the navy yard at Washington when Fort Sumter was fired upon. He at once resigned his commission in the Navy. Later, however, when he learned that Maryland was not seceding, he tried to recall his resignation. When his request was refused, he joined the Confederate Navy and the rank of Admiral of the Navy was created for him.

Because Buchanan was disabled in the battle between the *Virginia* and the *Monitor*, he was replaced by another officer—Captain Josiah Tattnall of the "blood is thicker than water" incident in Chinese waters.

Captain A. F. Warley, in command of the Confederate ram *Manassas* which, as we shall see later, tried to sink the *Mississippi* in the Battle of New Orleans, had been one of the *Mississippi's* officers before the firing on Fort Sumter.

And so it went. In some cases, officers were asked to leave the service of the United States Navy simply because, as southerners, their loyalty was suspected. One such was Captain Stribling, Flag Officer of the East India Squadron, who was a South Carolina man, but in his case the Navy probably made a mistake, for though he went home he did not join the Confederate Navy.

One who did not resign, and whose loyalty to the United States of America was never doubted, was David Farragut, a Tennessee man, who from the outbreak of war, in his forthright fashion, let both the North and the South know exactly how he stood—foursquare for the United States of America, and against secession.

It was under Farragut that George Dewey served in his first engagement, and the older man became the hero of the younger. "Farragut has always been my ideal of the naval officer, urbane, decisive, indomitable," Dewey wrote in his autobiography. "Whenever I have been in a difficult situation, or in the midst of such confusion of details that the simple and right thing to do seemed hazy, I have often asked myself, 'What would Farragut do?' "

A few days after the firing on Fort Sumter, George Dewey, on furlough in Montpelier, received orders to report for duty on the steam frigate *Mississippi*, which, as Perry's flagship, had already made naval history in Japanese waters, and had a bay near Yokohama named after her. On May 10, 1861, Dewey joined his ship, then under the command of Captain T. O. Selfridge, who, having spent all of his adult life under sail, never seemed quite at ease on a ship with a tall black smokestack amidships, and seemed always a little unhappy as he watched the paddle wheels churning water and felt the vibration of the engine under his feet.

Since the South was not a manufacturing region, it depended on shipments of manufactured goods from Europe, and on shipments of its own cotton for money. One of the first objectives of the North, then, was the blockade of the extended coastline from Hampton Roads southward to Key West, and westward to Mexico. The *Mississippi*, when Lieutenant George Dewey joined her, was under orders to proceed to the Gulf of Mexico on blockade duty as part of a squadron under command of Captain John Pope. Pope, a veteran of the Navy who, along with the other elderly captains of the ships in the Gulf blockade, was unfamiliar with steam, seemed reluctant to enter an engagement with the enemy.

George's first sight of battle came when the Con-

The "Manassas"

federate ram *Manassas*, a tugboat converted into a vessel of war by being clothed with an iron prow with which to smash into wooden vessels, punched headlong into Pope's flagship, *Richmond*, and punctured her side, so frightening the commander and the rest of the squadron that a hurried retreat was called for. This episode, which hardly deserved to be called an engagement, called "Pope's Run" after the flag officer, was undoubtedly one of the reasons why Captain Pope was replaced by David Glasgow Farragut.

Perhaps it is not surprising that Farragut, though born in Tennessee, was loyal to the Union rather than to the Confederacy to which the state of his birth had seceded. He had been adopted in boyhood by the Boston-born naval officer David Porter, and served as midshipman under Porter on the *Essex*. At the time of his assignment to the Gulf Squadron Farragut was sixty years of age, but hale, and with no thought of retirement. His foster-brother David Dixon Porter, then forty-eight, was in command of a mortar boat flotilla that was later to take part, under Farragut, in the Battle of New Orleans.

Farragut's arrival in the Gulf was the signal for things to begin happening. The coast blockade was at least hampering the movement of cotton out of the South, and of manufactured goods into it. During the year 1861 the North Atlantic fleet had captured more than 150 privateers trying to run the blockade, and Flag Officer DuPont, after having destroyed the Confederate positions at Port Royal Sound in South Carolina had gained control of a long stretch of the Atlantic Coast. Intercourse between the South and Europe was being well disrupted. The southern part of the Mississippi River was in control of the South. This made it possible for the eastern states of the Confederacy and Louisiana, Arkansas, and Texas, lying to the west of that sprawling, meandering river, to be in constant touch with one another. It also made it impossible for the North to use that part of the river to transport Union troops and supplies.

Abraham Lincoln said that he wanted to see the Mississippi "flow unvexed to the sea." But before this could be achieved there were several Confederate strongpoints whose guns had to be silenced—Fort Jackson, on the west bank, and Fort St. Philip, on the east bank of the river, about 30 miles above the gulf; New Orleans, the metropolis of the South, 170 miles above the mouth of the river; Port Hudson, which guarded the essential Confederate supply route through the Red River; and Vicksburg.

To achieve this, Secretary of the Navy Gideon Welles, and his assistant Gustavus Fox, planned an attack on the river strongholds and on New Orleans itself by the Gulf squadron under Farragut, while a number of gun boats were to work their way down the river.

Shortly after Farragut's arrival in the Gulf, Captain

Selfridge of the *Mississippi* was replaced by Captain Melancthon Smith. Meanwhile in December, 1861, a law had been passed retiring all naval officers at the age of sixty-two, or after forty-five years of service. Consequently, many captains were dropped and officers were shifted from ship to ship. On board the *Mississippi*, six officers senior to George Dewey were shifted to other ships. Thus Dewey, at twenty-four, ranked next to the captain and became executive officer.

When older officers on other ships complained that the young man outranked them, Farragut went to Captain Smith and told him about it, suggesting that an older officer be transferred to the *Mississippi* to act as executive. But Smith would not hear of it.

"Dewey is doing all right," he said. "I don't want a stranger here."

David Farragut's flagship, the "Hartford"

"Then we will let him stay," Farragut answered.

George Dewey was always to remember Farragut and Smith with respect and affection. The two men had much in common. Both were deeply religious and had an unswerving faith in Providence and the righteousness of the Union cause. Both were fearless, and both had an uncompromising sense of fairness.

Dewey tells two stories illustrating Captain Smith's moral principles. After the Battle of New Orleans, Smith saw Dewey take a glass of champagne in the house of a Union officer.

"Dewey, do you drink champagne?" he asked.

"Yes," Dewey answered, "when it's as good as this."

"If I had known that," Captain Smith said, "I do not think that I should have had so much confidence in you."

On another occasion, hearing the men on the ship swearing lustily over a particularly exasperating job, he ordered Dewey to have all the crew "lay aft." When they were gathered there, the captain stood before them soberly for a moment, then said,

"Hereafter any officer caught swearing will be out under suspension, and any man caught swearing will be put into double irons."

George Dewey thought none the less of his captain for this attitude. It was one in which he had grown up under his father, and he rather welcomed the restraint that had been imposed on his own speech and that of the men. The two men worked together excellently, with mutual respect and confidence. During battle, Smith was the personification of energy, but at other times he left the running of the ship to his executive, George Dewey.

The three officers—Farragut, Smith, and Dewey—were a striking sight as they met on Farragut's visits to the *Mississippi*. The sixty-year-old Farragut was clean-shaven, (in a day when most men wore mustaches and many wore beards as well), broad-shouldered, straight as a ramrod, with a large head that baldness had not yet touched, firm, thin, lips and clear eyes that inspired confidence, yet would put fear into the heart of the guilty. Anyone looking closely at photographs of Farragut and Dr. Julius Dewey, George's father, could not fail to see a certain slight resemblance between them, in the high forehead that each had, the thin-lipped mouth, and the general shape of the face. There were traits of character that the two shared also: a deep religious faith; an unswerving sense of responsibility; a kindliness, yet firmness in discipline. It is not unlikely that this resemblance to the father who, all of his life, had such an influence on George, was one reason for the deep respect and affection in which he held Farragut.

Smith, younger than Farragut, was somewhat stockier, with beard and mustache, and a shock of heavy black hair, surmounting a kindly face with eyes that had a glint of humor in them. George Dewey, who later was to become portly, was at this time a slim young man, looking somewhat older than his twenty-four years, but still almost a boy beside his two superior officers. From the point of view of facial adornment he had chosen the middle way

At left: David Farragut; at right, Melancthon Smith

between Farragut's clean-shaven face and Smith's full
beard and mustache. Dewey wore the mustache that he
had started at Annapolis, but no beard.

There were differences in age—between Farragut and
Dewey, thirty-six years—differences in background, differences in authority. While Farragut and Smith talked, the
young executive remained silent unless one of his superiors
addressed him, and then spoke modestly and briefly.

But binding these three men together was a common
respect, each for both of the others, a common courage, a
common loyalty to the United States of America and the
ideals for which it stood, and a determination to imple-
ment Abraham Lincoln's resolve to "preserve the union."
They were a trio who understood one another and who
fought together as a team.

Chapter 5
The Battle of New Orleans

When we think of the Civil War, we are apt to remember such battles as Bull Run, Gettysburg, and Antietam. The war between the northern and southern units of the temporarily disunited states of America is usually thought of as a land war as, indeed, to a large extent it was.

Yet no less important was the naval action, some of it at sea, and much of it on the Mississippi River. The control of this mighty stream was, from the very outset of the war, a matter of bitter concern to both the North and the South. To the North, the river formed a great natural highway and line of communication, and being able to send northern ships down it freely would cut off the Confederacy from the resources of Arkansas, Louisiana, and Texas. To the South it was of the utmost importance to prevent the very objectives of the North.

For over two years after the fall of Fort Sumter the battle for the great waterway was waged, to be finally decided at Vicksburg and Port Hudson in July, 1863. This was more than a year after New Orleans had fallen to the North and two years after the hotly disputed question of whether or not Missouri would secede had been won by the anti-secessionists and thus St. Louis had been preserved to the Union.

Moving quickly, at the outset of the war, Brigadier General U.S. Grant had secured Cape Girardeau, Missouri, and also fortified it, and Cairo, Illinois, and points farther south. Memphis, Tennessee, was not fortified.

Thus, at the time that the advance against New Orleans from the Gulf of Mexico was planned, the Mississippi was, to all intents and purposes, under control of the North as far south as Vicksburg, and held by the South from Vicksburg to the Gulf. The task set for Farragut's squadron was to open the river in order to join forces with those from the North and free the entire length of the river from rebel control.

The attack on New Orleans had, of course, been anticipated by the South, and preparations had been made to destroy, if possible, any ships that tried to reach the city. Forts Jackson and St. Philip were heavily armed, and across the river, under their guns, was stretched a heavy chain supported by several old hulks. Between the forts and New Orleans, earthworks and batteries were installed in every bayou and bend of the river. In New Orleans itself a garrison of at least 10,000 troops was stationed, and nearby the South's river fleet, consisting of twelve ships, waited expectantly. "Our only fear," said a New Orleans paper in an April editorial, "is that the Northern invaders may not appear. We have made such extensive preparations to meet them that it were vexatious if their invincible armada escapes the fate we have in store for it."

These facts were, of course, in general known to Farragut, and he was aware that no easy victory awaited.

It was an oddly assorted fleet that the North was preparing for battle. There were the big screw sloops *Hartford* (Farragut's flagship), *Richmond*, *Pensacola*, and *Brooklyn*, the side-wheeler *Mississippi*, the screw corvettes *Oneida*, *Varuna*, and *Iroquois*, nine screw gunboats of five hundred tons, known as "the ninety-day boats," because they had been built in that time, a mortar flotilla, under the command of Farragut's foster-brother, David Porter, and a number of ferry boats and other miscellaneous craft.

There was some delay in the movement of the fleet upriver. The *Pensacola* and the *Mississippi*, both sea-going vessels, were heavier than any other ships that had ever made their way into and up the Mississippi, and could not, by their own power get over the bar at the river's mouth. And so, after the rest of the fleet was in the river, the task of getting these two ships to join the fleet was undertaken.

George Dewey supervised the lightening of the *Mississippi*. Most of her spars and rigging were removed, and the coal bunkers were emptied. Every day the ships' boats would bring a day's supply of coal from the collier. Tow lines were attached to boats of Porter's mortar flotilla and eventually both the *Mississippi* and the *Pensacola* were dragged through a foot of mud and joined their sister ships.

Now the initial softening-up process began. Porter, who had camouflaged his twenty mortar boats by attaching tree branches to their masts, moved them into position close to the wooded bank of the river. Here they could not be seen by the men who manned Forts Jackson and St. Philip. On the eighteenth of April, 1862, the day after all of Farragut's fleet had assembled in the river, Porter opened fire on the forts with his thirteen-inch mortars. All night long, George Dewey, from the motionless *Mississippi*, could see the mortar shells rise, at intervals of about ten minutes, their graceful loops in the air outlined by the burning fuses, and drop into the forts.

The men on the ships were so busy that there was not much time for sleep, yet so dog-tired all the time that when they did lie down they slept like logs. On every ship there was feverish activity of preparation for the ascent of the river and the assault on New Orleans. The ships were "trimmed by the head," that is, loaded heaviest in the bow so that if they went aground it would be forward. In the swift current of the river, any ship that grounded aft would turn its head downstream, which was to be avoided. Wherever possible, guns were mounted on the poops and forecastles, and howitzers in the tops, with iron shields to protect the gunners.

Around each gun the decks of the ships were whitewashed so that the gunners could see to serve them better at night. Not one of the Union ships was armored, and, in order to give them some protection from shells, anchor chains were hung along their sides. On the *Mississippi*,

Lieutenant Dewey had chains stored in the coal bunkers between the side wheels and the boilers and machinery. The sides of the vessels were daubed with mud to make them less visible—forerunner of the elaborate camouflage that was later used in World War I.

All of these preparations were overseen by Farragut himself who went from ship to ship in one of the *Hartford's* boats, rowed by sailors. There was scarcely a night when the flagship did not signal for boats to tow fire rafts to a point where they could not menace any of the fleet.

The fire rafts were among the devices that the South had concocted with which to bedevil the northern ships. They were old hulks which, soaked with tar and resin, were set afire and then turned loose to float downstream. If one of them were to rest alongside a ship even for a few minutes it would set fire to it. Launches from the northern ships threw grapnels into the burning hulks, towed them to shore, made them fast there, and left them to burn out.

Another group of pestilential southern crafts were the rams, of which the *Manassas* was the most famous. The rams and the fire rafts were especially troublesome during the river campaign.

During the night of April 20, Lieutenant Caldwell, commanding the "ninety-day" gunboat *Itasca*, and Lieutenant Crosby commanding another, the *Pinola*, both with their masts removed, so that it was difficult to distinguish them from the hulks that anchored the chain above the forts, slipped quietly upstream. At the same time Porter's gunners bombarded the forts so thoroughly that there were often eight or nine shells in the air at once. After some difficult maneuvering, Caldwell got above the chain barrier; then turning, with the current to help him, charged the chain with a full head of steam. The chain snapped, the hulks swung downward with the current, and there was a gap large enough to permit every vessel in Farragut's fleet to go through.

On the night of April 23 there was no sleep for Lieutenant George Dewey. He knew that the chain barrier had been breached; he knew that everything had been done aboard the *Mississippi* that could be done to make her ready for battle; for he had himself seen to the preparations. He knew that the gun crews had been drilled insistently day after day in order to insure a smooth efficiency in loading and firing. All was in readiness, and every man aboard the ship was in a state of nervous excitement waiting for the signal for action.

Captain Melancthon Smith of the *Mississippi* had been against Farragut's plan to make the initial attack on the forts at night, favoring a bold dash in daylight, at full speed, and with all the fire power the fleet could command, pointing out that thus the heavy draught vessels would run much less danger of going aground in unfamiliar waters. But Farragut had other ideas.

At midnight of April 23 a long-drawn breath and a sharp "ah" from Captain Smith made George Dewey turn quickly to see two red lights at the peak of Farragut's flagship, the *Hartford*. This was the prearranged signal for the fleet to get underway. Immediately the *Pensacola,* without lights, a deeper shadow against the dark of the river's bank, began to move slowly upstream. The *Pensacola* had heavier armament than any other ship in the fleet, and led the advance. The *Mississippi* followed the *Pensacola* in the first division under the command of Flag Officer Bailey; Farragut, in the *Hartford*, led the second division of the attack, which, it was expected, would take the brunt of the fire from the forts, since it was hoped that the first division would escape notice in the night.

As soon as the signal was seen, Captain Smith turned to Dewey and said, "I can't see in the night. I'm going to leave that to you, Dewey. You have younger eyes."

Smith took charge of the battery while Lieutenant Dewey, with a sudden surge of excitement, and wondering whether he was capable of discharging the responsibility thrust upon him, took up his post on the hurricane deck from which the ship was handled. If there was a tremor under his calm exterior it would not have been surprising. He was, after all, only twenty-four and was about to face the fire of an enemy in a situation in which the enemy had the advantage. Also the responsibility had suddenly been thrust upon him of seeing that one of the Navy's finest fighting ships accounted for herself well.

But he had little time to consider his feelings. All of the fleet was without lights—gray shadows that were barely distinguishable. Collisions must be avoided, and the *Mississippi*, with its heavy draught, must be kept from running aground in the shoals of an unfamiliar river that Dewey had never navigated. Also she must keep her prescribed distance from the *Pensacola*, while the booming of the howitzers punctuated the advance.

As the *Pensacola* came abreast of the forts, the enemy discovered her, and Dewey, from his position on the hurricane deck of the *Mississippi*, close behind her, could hear the Confederate officers' orders to their gunners to fire. Then come a broadside which the *Pensacola*, stopping, answered with one of her own. At first this seemed to demoralize the enemy, but, as the *Pensacola* proceeded upstream, the fire from the fort was reopened. Once more the *Pensacola* stopped and fired broadsides, compelling the *Mississippi* also to stop. Once more the fire from the fort was silenced momentarily, only to be resumed almost immediately. It was clear that the entire Union fleet would have to pass through a heavy bombardment in order to get upstream.

Now the *Mississippi* was also under fire and returning it effectively under the orders of Captain Smith, while George Dewey was fully engaged in keeping his ship astern of the *Pensacola*.

He had almost forgotten a gentleman named Waud, an intrepid artist on the staff of an illustrated weekly magazine. Waud had asked Farragut for permission to accompany the fleet, and the flag officer had assigned the artist to the *Mississippi*. When the man had asked where he would be able to see the most action, Captain Smith had said laconically, "The foretop," and up the man had scrambled to stand beside a howitzer and the crewman who served it.

Dewey was suddenly aware of their visitor when the latter called down to him, "Here is a queer looking customer on our port bow!"

Looking toward the port side, the lieutenant saw what looked like the back of a huge lead-colored turtle. But Dewey knew this turtle, and knew that it had a stinger in its snout. He recognized it at once as the ram *Manassas*. He knew too that the ship was commanded by A. F. Warley, who had formerly been an officer on the *Mississippi,* and so was aware that her most vulnerable spot was just forward of the paddlewheel. It was obviously

The location of the ships; the enemy had the advantage

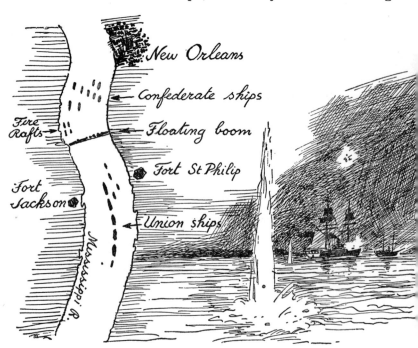

toward this spot that Warley was aiming the lethal nose of his strange craft.

Dewey's orders had been to keep in line directly behind the *Pensacola;* had he wished to do otherwise his proper procedure under ordinary circumstances would have been to consult Captain Smith. But the captain was below with the batteries. In less than half the time it would have taken Dewey to get word to him the *Manassas* would have been able to ram a hole in the *Mississippi* that would undoubtedly have put the northern ship out of the fight. Without hesitation George Dewey showed evidence that

The "Manassas" dashed in again

he could, in an emergency, disobey orders as well as follow them. He immediately gave the order to starboard the helm with the intention of ramming the rammer, knowing that if he could strike the *Manassas* head on, the superior weight of the *Mississippi* would sink her. But Warley knew this also, and, in addition, knew that his small craft could be turned much more quickly and in much smaller space than could the *Mississippi*. So he veered off easily, avoiding the hulk of the larger ship, and then, like a tiny hummingbird darting at the head of a blue jay, dashed in again, striking a glancing blow just aft of the *Mississippi's* port paddle wheel.

Looking over the side of the boat, Dewey could see the shining ends of some fifty copper bolts, which had been sheered off as if cut with a knife, as a section of timber 7 feet long, 4 feet broad, and about 4 inches deep had been torn away. Any other ship in the fleet would have been sunk by such damage as this, but the timbering of the *Mississippi* was so thick at this point that little harm had been done.

Now the *Manassas* slipped slowly downstream under the fire of the ships of Farragut's fleet, and managed, by a direct thrust, to put a superficial hole in the *Brooklyn*. Fortunately, the anchor chains, with which the ship had been protected, kept the damage from being serious.

Throughout the night the flashes from the guns and the flaming fire rafts cast a lurid glow over the river. Lieutenant Dewey, watching aft to see what progress the second division of ships was making, as well as forward in order to keep in line with, yet not overrun, the *Pensacola*, saw that the ships in the rear were pretty well out of formation. Each vessel was firing at will and trying to slip past the forts as quickly as possible. The *Brooklyn* and the *Hartford*, with Farragut aboard, were receiving a terrific cannonade, but answering it in kind.

As Dewey watched, he saw, to his horror, that one of the fire rafts, pushed by a little tug called the *Mosher*, was lodged directly against the *Hartford*, and that the flagship was in flames.

Later, with the typical generosity to a foe that was one of George Dewey's finest attributes, he wrote of the *Mosher's* commander, Captain Sherman:

"To him belongs the credit of one of the most desperate strokes of heroism I have ever known. It is an example of how the South, with its limited resources, was able to maintain its gallant struggle for four years against great odds. His tug had no guns and no armor. In the face of certain destruction from the guns of the *Hartford*, he pushed the raft against the *Hartford's* side. The *Mosher's* captain and crew all lost their lives, as far as is known, but they had the satisfaction of seeing flames darting up the *Hartford's* rigging and bursting through the ports, which, thanks to the discipline of the crew, were quenched."

It was dawn before the ships of Farragut's fleet had managed to pass the forts and what was left of the chain barrier, and take stock. On the *Mississippi*, two men had been killed and a few more wounded. The little *Iroquois* had been swept in the melee alongside the Confederate

Louisiana, still unfinished and without engines, but a heavily armed, motionless, floating fort. Her merciless fire accounted for thirty-two casualties on the *Iroquois,* though the northern ship herself managed to escape without too great damage. There were eleven casualties aboard the *Pinola,* and the *Varuna,* victim of a southern ram, was hard ashore, sunk to her top-gallant forecastle. She was the North's only loss, though three of the gunboats in the third division had failed to pass the obstruction.

But the bulk of Farragut's fleet had passed both the forts and the chain obstruction and had a comparatively clear passage to New Orleans, even though Forts Jackson and St. Philip had not surrendered and were still formidable obstacles to other ships attempting to sail up the river from the Gulf. It looked as though this phase of the advance upon New Orleans was over.

However, the intrepid Commander Warley of the *Manassas* had other ideas. The *Mississippi* was far upstream beyond the obstruction, and Captain Smith and Lieutenant Dewey were standing together on the hurricane deck in the dim light of morning, taking stock of the damage to their ship and to others around them. The faces of both were grimed with the smoke of battle, and the circles under their eyes told of the strain under which they had been all night long. Both were looking forward to a wash and a few hours of well-earned rest.

But they were not yet to leave the battle. Looking aft, Captain Smith saw the gray turtleback of the *Manassas* quietly headed upstream and toward them, apparently intent on finishing the job it had begun during the night. Nearby was a gunboat that Smith mistook, in the uncertain morning light, for the flagship of Flag Officer Bailey and shouted at it, "I want permission to run down the ram."

When he did not receive an answer he saw that he had mistaken the identity of the ship and was about to take matters into his own hands, as Dewey had under similar conditions the night before, but just at that moment the *Hartford* steamed past, her side blackened and still smoking from the fire that had been started in her the night before. High in the rigging, his favorite position aboard ship, stood Farragut, his face so blackened with smoke that he was scarcely recognizable, his voice hoarse from the commands he had shouted during the night.

"Run down the ram!" he shouted.

"Yes sir!" Smith called back eagerly. Then, turning to Dewey, he asked, "Can you turn the ship?"

"Yes sir," Dewey said, no less eagerly, and yet it was one of the least certain answers he had ever given to a question. The river was narrow at this point and George Dewey was completely unacquainted with its depths and shoals. However, he knew that he would turn his ship or run her aground in the attempt, and immediately gave the order. The helmsman spun the wheel, while George Dewey held his breath and then breathed a deep sigh of relief as he saw the nose of his ship pointed directly at the ugly turtle-like shell of the *Manassas*, as though to rip through her very belly.

But Warley, too, was a good sailor, and quickly turned the *Manassas*, avoiding his attacker, but at the same time running his own vessel into a mudbank where she stuck fast. Two broadsides from the *Mississippi* made the ram both unserviceable and untenable, and her crew came scrambling out of the forward hatch and hurried ashore to escape into the woods. A member of the *Mississippi's* crew went aboard to obtain Captain Warley's diary and other papers. Another set the *Manassas* afire. Then the crew of the *Mississippi* watched her as she finally floated free and, after drifting downstream a short distance, blew up and sank. Thus ended the career of one of the South's most valiant vessels.

The battle had begun at 2 A.M. Five hours later Farragut's ships were anchored above the forts, leaving behind only three southern ships that had survived the battle. Of the northern crews, 39 had been killed and 171 wounded.

That day the ships steamed upriver to within fifteen miles of New Orleans, their tired crews knowing that the city was theirs for the taking. There they anchored for the night, but still the weary men of the Union fleet had to fend off the fire rafts floating down the channel.

The next morning they proceeded toward the city, silencing two minor forts, Chalmette and McGehee, which fired on them as they passed.

Long before the buildings of the city could be seen, its location was clearly marked by columns of smoke that rose from storehouses which the Confederates had fired to keep them from falling into the hands of the Union conquerors. Soon Farragut's fleet was anchored abreast of the city, where the northern men found that everything which might have been of military value to them had been destroyed, including the almost finished and formidable ironclad, also named *Mississippi*, that was on the way. This and the unfinished, but well-armed, *Louisiana*, which had given a good account of herself during the fighting before the forts, would have made a considerable difference in the strength of the southern naval forces had they ever been completed and put into service.

Now, with New Orleans open for occupation at will by the northern forces, Farragut sent the *Mississippi* and the *Iroquois* downstream again to arrange for the capitulation of the forts and the *Louisiana*. Though they had not surrendered, their position was quite untenable, and final terms were arranged through Captain David Porter.

Again, as with Captain Warley of the *Manassas*, George Dewey saw, at first hand, results of the bitter conflicts that had assailed United States Army and Navy officers from the South.

Among the Confederate ships, which had been engaged in the river battle, was the *McRae*, commanded by Thomas B. Huger, whose service before the outbreak of war had been on board the *Iroquois*. During the river battle his ship had been engaged by the *Iroquois*, and Huger had been mortally wounded. He was succeeded in command by Charles W. Read, from Mississippi, who had been at Annapolis with George Dewey. Now "Savey"

Read, as he had been called at Annapolis, the conquered, came aboard the *Mississippi*, vessel of the conquerors, to ask his old schoolmate "Shang" Dewey for permission to take his dying captain and the other wounded from the *McRae* to New Orleans.

This was in the days when there was still a certain amount of chivalry in warfare, and gallant courtesy between respected foemen, and the permission was granted. (Later "Savey" Read roved up and down the Atlantic coast, an embarrassment and hazard to northern shipping, and was finally taken prisoner off the coast of Portland, Maine.)

A few days later General Butler quietly entered New Orleans with federal troops, and the battle of New Orleans was over. It is true that the Mississippi did not yet quite "flow unvexed to the sea" as Abraham Lincoln had said that he hoped it would. The guns of Port Hudson and Vicksburg must be silenced before the longed-for day arrived. But from the Gulf of Mexico to New Orleans, northern ships could now move freely, and plans were afoot for freeing the upper reaches of the river.

Two things were never to be forgotten by George Dewey. In later years he was to receive such honors as are awarded to few men. But it is doubtful if any were sweeter to him than the words of commendation that followed his first battle, when he was only twenty-four years of age.

In Captain Melancthon Smith's report to David Farragut on the part the *Mississippi* had played in the battle, he made special mention of one member of his staff—and of only one.

"I have much pleasure," he wrote, "in mentioning the efficient service rendered by Executive Officer George Dewey, who kept the vessel in her station during the engagement, a task exceedingly difficult from the darkness and thick smoke that enveloped us from fire of our own vessels and the burning gunboats."

And there was a general commendation from an even more important source. On May 14, President Abraham Lincoln, issued the following message to the Congress of the United States:

"Believing that no occasion could arise which would . . . be more pregnant with happy influence as an example I cordially recommend that Captain D. G. Farragut receive a vote of thanks of Congress for his services and gallantry displayed in the capture, since 21st December, 1861, of Forts Jackson and St. Philip, the City of New Orleans, and the destruction of various rebel gunboats, rams, etc."

There followed a list of officers commanding the northern vessels that were engaged in the battle, with the recommendation that each be commended especially by name.

Since George Dewey was not actually in command of the *Mississippi* his name was not, of course, on the list, though Melancthon Smith's was. But though Dewey would never have said this himself, he knew that he had earned some of President Lincoln's commendation, and he walked the deck of the good ship *Mississippi* a little taller.

Chapter 6

Port Hudson and Vicksburg

For nearly twelve months the *Mississippi* and the *Pensacola*—both of which were considered to be of too heavy draft to go upriver with Farragut past Vicksburg, Mississippi—were left behind as guard ships at New Orleans. The Mississippi River was now open to Union traffic from the gulf to New Orleans, and from the North to Vicksburg. But while Port Hudson, Louisiana, between New Orleans and Vicksburg, and Vicksburg remained in Confederate hands, supplies from western Louisiana and Texas could pour into Mississippi and northern Louisiana through the Red River, which joined the Mississippi just north of the boundary line between these two states.

Action against both points was begun late in 1862 when Grant and Sherman converged on Vicksburg, but were repulsed, and Major General N. P. Banks relieved General Butler at New Orleans and began to lay plans for an assault by land upon Port Hudson.

Meanwhile the *Mississippi* and the *Pensacola* marked time in the harbor of New Orleans, while its officers found what social life they could among the few loyal Unionists in the city. Most of the population of the city were openly hostile, and many were saying that they would still drive the Yankees into the river.

During the tenure of General Butler, George Dewey had occasion to perform a service to a well-meaning, loyal son of the Confederacy, and did so with splendid tact.

A forging on one of the *Mississippi's* paddle wheels had been broken. The only place nearby where a new one could be made was the Confederate foundry and ship-works which had been constructing the Confederate iron-clads *Louisiana* and *Mississippi* when the battle of New Orleans had interrupted the work. But the owner of the works refused positively to serve a Yankee ship. When the matter was reported to General Butler, he promptly ordered the man arrested and sent to Fort Jackson.

After the man had been taken into custody, his wife came aboard the *Mississippi* and asked to see Captain Smith. She had been afraid to go to General Butler, she said, for all of New Orleans thought of him as a monster, but she had heard that Captain Smith was a gentleman. Her husband, she told him, was in very poor health, and confinement in Fort Jackson would almost certainly kill him. He would make the forging if he were released. Wouldn't Captain Smith intercede with General Butler on the man's behalf?

Captain Smith said that he had no desire whatever to see the man imprisoned, he was really only interested in having his ship repaired, and turned over the diplomatic task of interviewing the general to young George Dewey,

who, knowing the crusty old fellow's reputation, under-
took it with some misgivings.

Dewey found the general at his desk, in full uniform,
with his sword on and two loaded pistols lying ready to
hand on the desk in front of him, for he had heard rumors
that there was a plan to assassinate him.

George Dewey put the case to him as favorably as
possible, emphasizing the great need of the *Mississippi* for
the casting, the impossibility of getting it made at any
nearby foundry save that of the man now incapable of
making it because he was under arrest, the understand-
ability of the man's loyalty to the cause to which his state
was committed, and his own conviction that the iron-
worker was now ready to do the job that was asked of
him and to do it well, if he were given his freedom.

General Butler was convinced, and George Dewey
hurried from his office with a note authorizing the prisoner's release. He reached the wharf just in time to take
him off the boat before it cast off for Fort Jackson.

In the spring of 1863, Grant and Sherman again
pressed toward Vicksburg. Banks's instructions had been to
co-operate with the attack on Vicksburg, proceeding from
New Orleans to aid Grant and Sherman, and taking Port
Hudson on the way. But, knowing the strength of the
Port Hudson defenses, Banks decided that he had not
enough forces to take it.

It was indeed a formidable strongpoint. The parapets
around it had an average thickness of 20 feet, and the
depth of the ditch below the top of the parapet was not

less than 15 feet. Twenty siege guns were mounted along the bluff about 80 feet above the river. The land defenses consisted of a continuous parapet beginning at Ross's Landing, about a mile below Port Hudson, running eastward for about a mile, thence northward, and finally westward again to meet the river about half a mile north of Port Hudson. Whether the approach was made from the river or from the land side, the taking of Port Hudson, and for that matter Vicksburg, was obviously going to be no easy matter. Efforts to blockade both ports with individual gunboats had failed, and Farragut saw that in order to give Grant and the land forces the aid they needed the Red River supply route must be blocked.

One promising operation undertaken in early February was an expedition across the Yazoo Peninsula in Mississippi in which the Army and the Navy both took part. Army engineers flooded an abandoned barge canal known as the Yazoo Pass by blasting the levee. Through this Porter and Grant planned to send an expedition into the upper Yazoo River, consisting of several ironclads and thirteen army transports, which could cut off Vicksburg from supplies through the Yazoo Delta, while the Army could besiege the strongpoint from the rear.

Confederate spies stationed in Helena, Arkansas, however, reported on the operation and a working party of Negroes was sent to fell large trees across the route. Some of these were pushed out of the way by the ironclads. Others were so stubborn that they had to be hauled out of the way, and it was necessary to send two hundred miles to Memphis for six-inch hempen rope strong enough to do the job. Overhanging trees impeded the tall troop transports and had to be cut away. A hastily erected Confederate fort harassed the Union expedition just before it reached the Yazoo and a week of indecisive fighting followed.

Meanwhile Porter had sent the *Queen of the West* and the *Indianola* from his headquarters at Milliken's Bend in an attempt to control the Mississippi from Vicksburg to Port Hudson. But both ships were captured by the Confederates.

Now a new attempt was made to approach Vicksburg through Steele's Bayou (opening into the Yazoo ten miles above its junction with the Mississippi), Black Bayou, Deer Creek, Rolling Fork, and Sunflower River, a roundabout way that would bypass Confederate obstructions. Into this unknown route Porter pushed with five turtle-backed ironclads, four mortars, and four tugs.

At the outset the deep and wide waters of Steele's Bayou offered easy passage. But as the flotilla made its way into Black Bayou, things became more difficult. Often the ironclads had to ram and uproot trees. At some of the bends the passage was so narrow that the boats negotiated them with the greatest difficulty, bumping into overhanging branches and often shaking loose snakes and lizards, which had taken refuge in them.

In Deer Creek the passage was wider and the stream passed through fertile plantations. Surprised plantation owners, recognizing the ships as invaders from the North, fired piles of cotton, waiting on wharves for shipment, and the ironclads had often to run the gauntlet between fiercely flaming heaps on both sides of the river.

But in spite of the enmity of the plantation owners and the possibility of punishment, cheering Negro slaves thronged the banks and ran along them shouting joyously. "Bless the Lord, I'm ready!," "De Lord and de abolishuns done set the darkeys free!," "Glory be to God!" The cries rang out clearly above the noise of the boats' engines.

In the upper stretches of Deer Creek, willow withes had to be cut under water, and the Negroes along the bank, all knowing they were risking severe punishment from their masters, helped with a will.

Both Farragut and Grant were learning that they must use every strategy and all of the strength at their command to free the points of the Mississippi still held by the South. Farragut decided that the lower Mississippi River fleet must now be taken past Port Hudson, and that even the *Mississippi* with its heavy draft must be included in the efforts.

As a result of this decision George Dewey often said in later years that during the Port Hudson operation he had lived about five years in one hour.

On March 14, 1863, the fleet anchored off Profit's Island, about seven miles below Port Hudson. There were four sloops of war, a river ironclad, and four gunboats, carrying a total of 121 guns. In addition there were five mortar schooners. To the side of each of the larger boats, except the *Mississippi*, which was a side-wheeler, a gunboat was lashed on the port side, which was the side that would not be exposed to the Port Hudson batteries. Thus each boat had some of the advantages of a boat with twin screw propellers. Not only did it have greater power, which would be most useful in case it ran aground, but also greater maneuverability, since by backing with one propeller and going forward with the other, it could turn in a much smaller space than was possible with one propeller.

A combined river and land operation had been planned. On the 14th, the day when Farragut's fleet had anchored off Profit's Island, 12,000 of Banks's troops took up positions to the east of the Port Hudson defenses, intending to make a demonstration against them by artillery fire and thus divert their attention from the passage of the fleet which was originally scheduled for the morning of the 15th. However, late in the afternoon of the 14th, Banks received a despatch from Farragut saying that he had decided to make the passage that evening and would start soon after dark. But the land troops were delayed by errors in their maps and the necessity to build some bridges and, beyond firing a few shots at Confederate pickets, accomplished nothing. Indeed Banks's men were still building bridges when, at 11:30 P.M., they heard the sound of Farragut's guns firing from the river.

All started off well. Each of the large boats had a river pilot, familiar undoubtedly with the deeps and shoals of the Mississippi, but accustomed to piloting ships built for river navigation rather than for the open sea where there was plenty of depth and plenty of room in which to turn.

At 10 P.M. the *Hartford* led off, followed by the *Monongahela* and the *Richmond*, with the *Mississippi* bringing up the rear.

All was silence at the outset—an unpleasant silence for those on the river who had expected to hear the guns of Banks's artillery firing from the land side—until the *Hartford* was past the first of the batteries. Then the darkness of the night was illuminated by the sudden flare and arching flight of a rocket fired from Port Hudson, a signal that the fleet had been seen, and the whole crest of the bluff was suddenly illuminated by the flashes of gunfire as all of the Confederate batteries let loose from their positions high above the northern fleet. Simultaneously piles of pitch-soaked cordwood were set aflame on the bank of the river opposite Port Hudson so that every ship in Farragut's fleet was clearly silhouetted for the Confederate gunners.

The gunfire from both the ships and Port Hudson was so heavy that a pall of smoke settled over the fleet, making it impossible to see anything but the flashes of the guns.

There followed an hour of confusion and near disaster. At a bend in the river the *Hartford* was caught by the current and swung around with her head toward the Confederate batteries and her stern aground. But with the help of her gunboat companion she got off, got her head pointed upstream again, and steamed out of range with one man killed and two wounded. Had the Confederate gunners depressed their guns sufficiently the loss would probably have been much greater.

Now as the *Richmond* came into range, the gunners of Port Hudson corrected their error, made a direct hit, which tore into the engine room, and by chance twisted the safety valve lever, thereby opening the valve so that she had no power. The *Genesee*, the gunboat lashed to her side, was unable to move the larger ship upstream unaided, and so there was nothing to do but turn about and retreat downstream. In the smoke and tumult of the battle, the *Richmond's* gunners did not know that the ship had been turned around and kept on firing. But now they were, of course, firing in the wrong direction. Mistaking the flashes of the *Mississippi's* guns for those of the Confederates, they were firing on their own ship, and the *Mississippi's* gunners on the other hand fired back at the *Richmond*, thinking they were firing on Port Hudson.

Next in line was the *Monongahela*, whose gunboat, the *Kineo*, had her rudder damaged by a shot, and the *Monongahela* ran aground, tearing loose the lines that bound her to the *Kineo*. Before she was freed, the bridge of the *Monongahela* was shot away from under her captain, McKinstry, and in the fall which he received he was incapacitated. The *Kineo* drifted downstream and the *Monongahela* proceeded alone upstream until a heated crank pin stopped her engines and she, too, had to drift downstream under fire, sustaining heavy casualties.

The *Mississippi*, bringing up the rear, passed the

Monongahela while she was aground, without either Captain Smith or Lieutenant Dewey seeing her. Under heavy fire, covered by a thick pall of smoke, the pilot was navigating the ship more by instinct than by landmarks. While they were passing the batteries, in what the pilot knew was shallow water, the ship proceeded very slowly and was under constant bombardment. The pilot was actually feeling his way toward a shoal that he knew lay ahead of them. When he thought they had passed it, he gave the order "Starboard the helm! Full speed ahead!" No one was unhappy to have that order obeyed, thinking that it would get the ship quickly out of the range of the Port Hudson batteries.

But as a matter of fact the pilot's order ran the ship, under a full head of steam, into the very shoal that he had been trying to avoid, and the *Mississippi* was fast aground, a sitting duck for the marksmen on the bluff at Port Hudson.

Now the long drills to which Captain Smith and Lieutenant Dewey had subjected the men of the ship off New Orleans came to their aid, for the discipline aboard ship was excellent. Every man stuck to his post as the engines were reversed and the gun crews continued to pour fire into the Port Hudson defenses, even though the barking of the guns, the pounding of the engines, and the noise of the paddle wheels combined to drown out commands. Over and over the ship was hit and the toll of the wounded and dead was continuously mounting, while the smoke hung so thickly over the vessel that it was difficult for the gun crews to see to serve the guns, or for one man to recognize another on deck.

For half an hour the engines worked under a full head of steam, trying to back the *Mississippi* off, but without budging her. Then George Dewey, hunting out Captain Smith on deck, peering into the begrimed face of every man he met, finally found his captain lighting a cigar as calmly as though the ship were still anchored off New Orleans.

"Well," the captain said calmly, "it doesn't look as though we could get her off."

"No," said George Dewey, "it does not," and waited for orders.

For a moment the captain stood in silence. While the two officers stood thus, a man came hurrying to them to report that the ship was on fire forward in the storeroom where there was a great deal of inflammable material.

Not until forty years later did George Dewey learn how the fire had started. By then the Civil War, though not forgotten, had receded so far into the past that Southerners and Northerners, once more united as one nation, could talk about events of the war as friends. In Palm Beach, Florida, Dewey met a man who had served in what was called a "hot shot battery" at Port Hudson. Here the round shot was heated red hot before being loaded into the cannons, with wads of wet hay or hemp between the shot and the powder, and then fired. It was one of these that had set fire to the *Mississippi*.

Now Captain Smith gave the order to throw the guns of the port battery overboard to lighten the ship while the fire in the storeroom was being fought, in the hope that the ship could be floated. But under the increasingly accurate firing from Port Hudson and the smoke that made the darkness almost absolute, the men did not succeed in getting the guns overboard, and Captain Smith had to face the heartbreaking decision to abandon his ship. He had, from the first, opposed fighting at night, and now night fighting had brought about the very disaster that he had feared.

"Can we save the crew?" he asked George Dewey.

"Yes sir," Dewey answered, no doubt adding in his mind, "Those who are left," for the number of dead was increasing rapidly.

He hastened to give the necessary orders. Not once had any of the batteries facing Port Hudson ceased firing. When there were casualties among the gun crews the places were at once filled by others. Dewey was later to remember how one of them, then Ensign Barker (later Rear Admiral Barker who took over command of the Asiatic squadron after the Spanish-American War), objected to leaving the ship.

Dewey found that all three of the boats on the starboard side had been smashed to bits by the enemy's fire. The three on the port side were still seaworthy and it was to these he turned with orders to load all of the seriously wounded into the first and send the boat downriver so that the injured could board one of the other ships and receive medical attention. The second and third boats were loaded with slightly wounded and unhurt members of the crew and ordered to make a landing on the bank and return at once for another load.

The boats took off with alacrity but it was so long before they returned that Lieutenant Dewey and Captain Smith became worried about them. The current was so swift at that point of the river that both officers knew that it would be impossible for the men to swim to shore. Meanwhile the Confederate guns of Port Hudson were continually pounding the stranded and wounded vessel.

Finally the boats arrived and, for the first time in the emergency, the crew's discipline began to break down as the remainder of the men aboard began to crowd and push each other in what was almost a panic, in an attempt to get aboard. One of the men rushed ahead, pushing his comrades aside, and attempted to jump into the boat ahead of the others. George Dewey calmly knocked him down with his fist, bringing him back to his senses. A few minutes later, when a wounded man slipped from the hands of the man who was lowering him into the boat and went into the river, the man whom Dewey had knocked down dove at once and pulled the wounded man to safety. It was quite typical of George Dewey that he now praised the man as wholeheartedly as he had punished him a few minutes before.

With the boats loaded for the second time there were still a number of men aboard the burning *Mississippi*, which shook with the shock of each Confederate shell that made a direct hit. However, the men were now under control and the panic had subsided. Yet their behavior, which had so nearly precipitated disaster by overcrowding the boats, made George Dewey realize why the boats had been so slow in returning from the first trip ashore. The men at the oars, acting under the impelling force of the instinct for self-preservation, had hesitated to return to the burning vessel that was a stationary target for the Confederate guns, in the fear that they might not be able to get off again. Realizing at the last moment that they might not return at all the second time, leaving those still aboard to a horrible death from the fire, George Dewey looked about for Captain Smith, intending to suggest that an officer go with the boats and make sure that they came back. Unable to find the captain in the smoke and confusion, Dewey swung himself down by the boat-falls and jumped into the stern of the second boat just as it pushed off. Not until the boat was too far away from the ship for him to get back onto it did he realize the chance he had taken of bringing disaster on his reputation. He, the second officer in command, had left his ship in distress with many of the crew still aboard her. He knew, as all men of the sea know, that in abandoning ship the captain must be the last man to leave the vessel, and the second officer, in this case George Dewey, the next to the last.

"That was the most anxious moment of my career," he wrote years later in his autobiography. "What if a shot should sink the boat? What if a rifle bullet should get me? All the world would say that I had been guilty of about as

craven an act as can be placed at the door of any officer."
As he did so often during his long career, he thought of
his father, and the good doctor's last words to him when
he had left the boy at Annapolis. "This would not be
pleasant reading for my father in Vermont," he wrote.
"He would no longer think that I had done 'the rest'
reasonably well. If the ship should blow up while I was
away and I should appear on the reports as saved, probably people would smile over my explanation."

Fortunately, however, though the boats were under
fire all the way to shore, no one was hit. As their bows
ground against the beach, the men scrambled out with a
will and started for cover. Dewey halted them with the
words, "All of you except four get to cover behind the
levee. Four of you will stay with me to go back to the
ship."

The men paused only long enough to hear his words
and then all continued their rush to the levee—with one
exception. The ship's cook, a powerful Negro, stood his
ground at attention before his officer.

"I'm ready to go back with you, sir," he said quietly.
It was as if he were saying "We, of the race who are
slaves, we for whose freedom you are fighting, know what
freedom is worth and are ready to fight for it, too."

Calling the men's attention to the cook's attitude,
Dewey soon had other volunteers for the boat by which
he stood. But only one man, named Chase, an acting master, stood ready by the other boat.

"Why don't you start back to the ship to get the rest of the officers and men?" Dewey asked.

"I can't get the men to man the boat," Chase answered.

Dewey said, "Use your revolver and see that your orders are obeyed."

Chase did so, and as the two boats got back to the *Mississippi*, George Dewey was as relieved as the men who had taken shelter behind the levee had been to get there. As soon as they were aboard, Captain Smith came to him, saying, "I have been looking all over for you. I was afraid you might have been killed."

Dewey explained where he had been and expressed his conviction that if he had not gone with the boats they would not have returned at all, and received no comment. Captain Smith had long since learned that his executive was able to make decisions of his own and act on them in emergencies, and had nothing but respect for this trait in the young man.

Now, with the two boats alongside and the remaining men of the crew in them, impatient to be away from the burning vessel, Captain Smith and his second officer set out on a search that George Dewey was never to forget. Up and down the decks they went, examining every prostrate figure to make sure that no spark of life remained in him, knowing how precious time was, yet fearful of leaving even one wounded man aboard, unable to move as the flames crept closer and closer to him. They kept calling loudly that this was the last chance to leave the ship, so that any who were living and conscious could call attention to their positions even if they were unable to move.

At one point Dewey was about to pass a group of bodies of men, all of whom seemed dead, when he thought that he saw a faint movement. Stooping down, he felt, more than saw, in the darkness, a youngster who was little more than a boy, wounded, and so faint that he could barely speak, lying under the body of a dead man. He was, of course, pulled out and carried tenderly to one of the boats.

Then Captain Melancthon Smith gave the last order he was ever to issue on board the gallant *Mississippi*. The ship was burning rapidly, but it still might have been possible, once she had been abandoned, for the Confederates to come aboard and salvage her for their own use. So the captain ordered that she be fired in another place to make sure of her complete destruction.

With Ensign O. A. Batchellor, George Dewey went below, carrying a lantern. Running to his stateroom, he took the mattress from his bed and ran with it to the ward room, which was the officers' mess room and sitting room. There he ripped open the mattress and put it under the oak dining table, piled chairs on top of it, and thrust the oil lantern into the inflammable mass. He and Batchellor also breached the stern of the ship, and then hurried back to the deck.

There four men got into the last boat, followed by

Ensign Batchellor, then Lieutenant Dewey, and, last of all, Captain Smith, in the strict tradition of seamanship, and the boats pushed off while the blaze that had been started in the wardroom shot up above the decks.

The Confederates, manning the Port Hudson fortifications, saw the sudden increase in the flames and, realizing what it meant, sent up a rebel yell that George Dewey was never to forget. "How they must hate us," he thought. Then he saw Captain Smith loosening the belt that carried his sword and two fine revolvers. As Dewey looked on in amazement the captain threw both revolvers and sword into the river.

"Why did you do that?" the young man asked.

"I'm not going to surrender them to any rebel," the captain answered laconically.

George Dewey did not follow his captain's example, and was glad later that he had not done so, for, although they were constantly shot at, the speed of the boat—with every man except Captain Smith and George Dewey pulling the oars for dear life—was so great that they were not hit, and soon they were safe around the bend and out of range. There they boarded the *Richmond*, which had earlier drifted downstream.

From this vantage point they watched sadly the last moments of the gallant *Mississippi*. Lightened by the burning of much of her superstructure, and with her stern weighted down by the water that had entered it, her bow was lifted sufficiently to float her and she swung around and drifted downstream, the flames leaping from her deck like dancing implements of destruction, lighting the banks on both sides of the river.

Her port guns were loaded and, as she passed the Confederate batteries, the heat reached the primers and one by one discharged them, "a dying ship manned by dead men, firing on the enemy," as Dewey put it. Some of the shots, it was said, took effect.

Captain Smith and his officers were watching in silence.

But George Dewey, with the rebel yell he had heard from Port Hudson still echoing in his ears, found some comfort in those final shots which the old vessel had hurled at the foe.

The flames lit the banks on both sides of the river

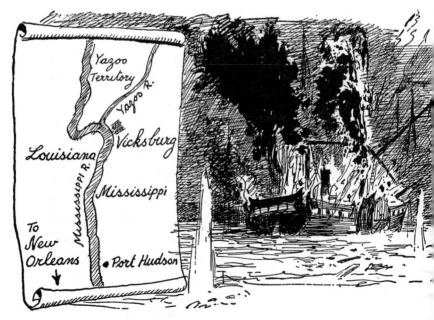

"She goes out magnificently anyway," he said to Captain Smith.

But the captain turned his face away, perhaps in order to conceal the look of anguish that darkened it.

"I don't think so," he said sharply.

A few minutes later the *Mississippi* went aground and exploded. Such was the end of a famous fighting ship which, in a sense, marked the transition from sail to steam in the United States Navy, and which had had a distinguished career.

Though all who had been a part of her crew mourned her loss, Farragut was philosophical about it. "You can't make an omelet without breaking eggs," he said. Far from being pleased by this remark, Captain Smith, who had

Soon they were safe around the bend and out of range

little sense of humor, remarked angrily, "He calls us an omelet!" But he felt better when he received letters of praise from Gideon Welles, Secretary of the Navy, and Assistant Secretary Fox, who wrote: "The noble ship has gone, but the Navy and the country have gained an example. However it was to be expected of him who in this war has done all things well."

Captain Smith was an honest man who refused to take all credit to himself when it should be shared with others.

"I consider that I would be neglecting a most important duty," he wrote in his report, "should I omit to mention the coolness of my executive officer Mr. George Dewey." Dewey later wrote that no word of commendation he had ever received was more precious to him than that which Captain Smith had given him after the Battle of Port Hudson.

Was the naval battle of Port Hudson a victory or defeat for the Union? In a sense it was a bit of both. Only the *Hartford* reached the upper river, but it served to aid the blockade of Vicksburg.

An officer without a ship, George Dewey was now sent to New Orleans as prize commissioner, where he had to judge disputes over cargoes captured in the blockade, and sell those declared legitimate prizes. The auctioneer who acted as his salesman, while a Southerner, had become a staunch abolitionist, and so a supporter of the Union cause, through the beauty of three octoroon slaves who, as he himself put it, were "whiter than his own daughter."

Revolted by the idea of putting them on the auction block, as he had been asked to do, he refused, and turned against the whole institution of slavery. Since to him, as to many, it seemed that the entire object of the Civil War was to free the slaves, his sympathies lay with the North.

Only for a few months did Dewey struggle with the task of turning prize cargoes into money for the Union government. Soon he was back on the river as executive officer of the sloop *Monongahela*, again under the captain for whom he had gained affection and respect aboard the *Mississippi*, Melancthon Smith. But only for a short time, since Smith was soon ordered north and Captain Abner Read took command of the vessel.

The *Monongahela* was stationed south of Port Hudson, and Farragut's flagship, the *Hartford*, was north of the strongpoint that was still held by the South, so when Farragut came south he used the *Monongahela* as his flagship, and Dewey saw a great deal of him. Usually Farragut's chief of staff, Captain Thornton A. Jenkins, was with him.

Generally speaking, the captain of a ship or the executive officer does not like to have his commander use the ship as a flagship, since, in a sense, it forces "company manners" on all of the officers at all times, and the captain himself never feels as though he were completely in control of his own vessel. But with Farragut it was different. He was so simple and friendly, so undesirous of any special honors due to his rank, so companionable, and so calm even when under fire, that he was always welcome, even though the *Monongahela's* quarters were somewhat crowded.

Farragut was an old-timer who loved the sea and the old days of sail. Dewey tells one pleasant story of him that illustrates this. As executive officer, the young lieutenant had ordered the officer of the deck to see that the ship had a thorough cleaning the first thing in the morning. The man to whom he issued the order was an old New England whaler, who had left the merchant service to enlist for the war. He was brown as a berry, gnarled and wrinkled, and wore small gold rings in his ears—a custom of sailors which had all but passed out of existence by Dewey's time.

The night was stiflingly hot and Dewey woke very early. At five o'clock, when the ship's activities should have begun, he heard no sound of holystones on the deck. He went above and found nothing whatever happening. In a hammock in the shade sat the old whaler with Farragut at his side.

"Why aren't you cleaning ship?" Dewey asked.

Before the other had a chance to reply Farragut spoke. With a smile, he said: "I'm afraid I'm to blame. We two veterans have been swapping yarns about sailing ship days."

Captain Read was a daring chap and a proud captain, who seemed more afraid of appearing cowardly than of danger from the enemy. His daring and pride cost him his life, and almost cost George Dewey his.

It was on a day when the *Monongahela* was steaming

upriver, escorting a small gunboat carrying ammunition for Banks's army. Suddenly a Confederate field battery, stationed at an embrasure in the levee nearby, opened fire on them. Captain Jenkins, who was aboard, suggested getting out of range at full speed. But Read had other ideas.

"I've never run from a rebel yet," he said, "and I'm not going to now."

Instead of running, he slowed the *Monongahela* and returned the fire of the rebel battery. With him on the quarterdeck stood Captain Jenkins and George Dewey.

Suddenly Dewey was blinded by a flash of fire and felt the stunning concussion of an exploding shell. As the air cleared, he was surprised to find that he was still erect and unhurt, but both Captain Read and Captain Jenkins were lying on the deck, the former bleeding profusely, and, as it turned out, mortally wounded, for he died the next day. The command now obviously fell to George Dewey and, without hesitation, he ordered "Full speed ahead," and the ship was soon out of range. Meanwhile Captain Jenkins was again on his feet. The explosion of the shell had merely hurled a cutlass at him from a rack of them on deck. Hitting him broadside, it had knocked him down and bruised him, but had not injured him seriously. George Dewey had, inexplicably, not received a scratch.

On July 4 Vicksburg surrendered. Five days later, Port Hudson was taken by General Banks. At last Lincoln's wish to see the Mississippi "flow unvexed to the sea" had been achieved.

Chapter 7
From Port Hudson to Fort Fisher

Technically George Dewey became commanding officer of the *Monongahela* as a result of Captain Read's death. But because of his youth he was transferred to the *Brooklyn*, a screw sloop, full rigged for sail in spite of her steam power, as executive under Captain Emmons.

From then until the end of the war he served on several ships. The first one, after the *Brooklyn*, was the *Agawam*, a wooden sidewheeler then being put into commission at the Portsmouth Navy Yard under the supervision of her skipper, Commander A. C. Rhind.

George Dewey was never to forget the months he spent at Norfolk, during which two notable events occurred. One was his meeting with Susie Goodwin, and the other was his civil arrest.

Susie was the daughter of Ichabod Goodwin, governor of New Hampshire, known as "Fighting Ichabod" because, at the outbreak of the Civil War, he had equipped troops at his own expense and sent them off to war. When George Dewey arrived at Portsmouth to become executive of the *Agawam*, Susie Goodwin was seen habitually in the

George and Susie Goodwin reach an "understanding"

company of Commander Rhind. But the younger George Dewey soon changed that, and before the *Agawam* left Portsmouth for the James River to become the flagship of Admiral S. P. Lee, there was an "understanding" between them.

Dewey's arrest grew out of the love of fighting that he had exhibited as a boy, and which never really left him, and out of his insistence upon having his orders obeyed. One day while the *Agawam* was being fitted out by civilian workmen, a hawser broke and the ship began to float away with the tide. Dewey, and members of the ship's crew who were standing by, made another line fast and tried to pull the ship back to dock, but needed help, and George, turning to a civilian workman named Garland who was standing idle, said, "Lend a hand here!"

Garland's answer was a laugh, the remark that he was not taking orders from any young naval officer, and continued indifference.

At this, Dewey's temper flared up and he knocked the man down with his fist. Garland got up, rubbed his face, and looked questioningly at Dewey. "I said 'lend a hand'," Dewey repeated, and the man took hold of the hawser and pulled with the rest.

A little later Deputy Sheriff George F. Plaisted appeared with a warrant for George Dewey's arrest, on Garland's complaint, and the young lieutenant, maintaining that he could not be arrested by a civil authority, followed Plaisted to the commandant of the yard who informed Dewey in no uncertain terms that he was wrong. George Dewey was tried on a charge of assault and fined $5.00 plus $8.00 costs.

"But," he said to his future father-in-law, Governor Goodwin, rubbing the knuckles of his fist and grinning, "it was worth it."

For a year, Dewey served as executive of the *Agawam*. During this time he saw a great deal of service on the James River, supporting General Butler's unsuccessful expedition toward Richmond. The most important engagement in which he took part during this time was at Four Mile Creek where his ship spent six days pounding the Confederate batteries. During the battle the only casualties aboard the ship resulted from an exploding shell on the quarterdeck that killed two men and wounded six.

But he never forgot the mosquitoes, which were savage and a constant annoyance, and the stuffiness of the ship in the intense heat. "In a sense," he reported later, "the fighting was the easiest part of the work." But perhaps his feeling arose partly from the fact that George Dewey always loved a good fight.

In September, 1864, Rear Admiral David D. Porter succeeded Rear Admiral Lee in command of the North Atlantic Squadron and sent for Dewey, wanting him to be executive officer of the *Minnesota*, a large steam frigate of the class of the *Wabash*. But the *Minnesota*'s captain had only to look at the slim figure, the youthfulness of whose face was not concealed by the mustache, to object that he was too young—he was only twenty-six—and he was sent back to the *Agawam*, for Porter knew that it was useless to give the captain of a ship an executive of whom he disapproved.

But Porter, still believing in the extraordinary abilities of this young man from Montpelier and knowing his record as executive of other ships, wrote to Assistant Secretary of the Navy Fox shortly after Dewey's twenty-seventh birthday, asking that the young man be assigned as executive officer of the *Colorado*, a ship of the same class as the *Wabash* and *Minnesota*, and in some respects, a problem ship. As a result, George Dewey participated in the culminating naval actions of the war, the two attacks on Fort Fisher.

The entire length of the Mississippi was now in

Union hands. Farragut, in the torpedo-infested waters of Mobile Bay, shouting "Damn the torpedoes, go ahead!" had wrested that harbor from the South in the most famous and the bloodiest naval battle of the war. Every port on the Gulf of Mexico now flew the Union flag. The Confederacy now had only two ports that a ship with a draft of over twelve feet could enter—Charleston in South Carolina and Wilmington in North Carolina, at the mouth of the Cape Fear River.

Charleston was well blockaded by some twenty Union vessels, but though more than thirty were usually on watch off Wilmington, blockade runners often slipped past them. The southern command, fully aware of the importance of keeping the port at least partially open, had sought to make Fort Fisher, at the mouth of the river, impregnable. They knew that if they lost both Charleston and Wilmington, with Sherman's army swinging northward and Grant's approaching Richmond, they would face the spring of 1865 without sufficient supplies to carry on the struggle.

A combined sea and land operation was now conceived by the North—to render Fort Fisher ineffective by naval fire and then land sea-borne troops under General Butler, who would take it by assault.

For this purpose the largest naval force that had yet been brought together during the war was assembled. It consisted of big frigates of the *Colorado* class, ironclads and monitors, and even merchant vessels transferred into gunboats. The *Colorado*, which previously had carried armament consisting of forty smooth bore guns now had one rifled 150-pounder, one 11-inch shell gun, and forty-six 9-inch shell guns.

But before the ship was fit to take part in a major engagement there was a job of revision to be done that was even more important than the strengthening of her armament, and it fell to young George Dewey to do it.

In spite of Dewey's youth, Commodore H. K. Thatcher, in command of the ship, welcomed him on board warmly, and told him at once that the ship was in very bad shape, particularly as to morale and discipline. He made it quite clear at the outset that Dewey had full authority in the government of the crew of over seven hundred men, who were quite obviously in need of a new conception of their duties. Dewey's predecessor, though he had the reputation of being a martinet, had never seemed to command the respect of the men or their obedience, even though the prison was always tenanted. At one time, shortly before Dewey had joined ship, more than a hundred members of the crew had been in irons at one time.

This seemed to George Dewey to be an intolerable situation. Further, he knew that the state of insubordination on board the ship had been basically the reason why Porter, knowing of Dewey's excellent relationship with the crews of the other ships on which he had served, had recommended him as its executive. Just as he had earlier determined not to disappoint his father, he now felt an obligation to live up to David Porter's expectations.

He knew that in any crew the troublemakers were in the minority. Most of the men, as in any group of human beings, were actually on the side of law and order, though some of them, through weakness, were easily led by the habitual complainers, the shirkers, and those who just plain seemed to enjoy stirring up trouble. Consequently Dewey decided to find out, as soon as possible, who the ringleaders of the insubordinate element were, and to deal with them promptly and decisively. He knew that if he did not prove to the crew at once that he was their master, they would master him.

The first test came quickly. On his first morning aboard the *Colorado*, the weather was cold and raw. Lieutenant Dewey called all hands on deck, but not all responded. It was explained by a junior officer that the weather was so cold that some of the men had refused to get out of their hammocks.

George Dewey did not turn over the job that had to be done to a subordinate officer, nor did he hesitate. He himself went among the hammocks, and wherever he found a man in one of them he tipped him out, quickly, roughly, and with no attempt to ease the fall that the man received. From that day on, when he called all hands on deck, all hands appeared on deck.

As he watched the men to find out which were the most consistent troublemakers, he discovered that the ringleader was a powerful Englishman named Webster. Much insubordination on the part of other members of the crew arose from their fear of retaliation from this brute of a

Any man found in a hammock was tipped out, roughly

fellow if they did not co-operate with his own infractions of discipline. Dewey watched Webster closely and took him into custody at his first breach of discipline. The prison was full, so Webster was put into irons in the hold.

A few days later Dewey heard the sound of breaking glass and the thuds of objects that were apparently being thrown about in the hold. An orderly came to him to report that Webster had broken loose, had driven his sentry from the hold in a rage, and was smashing bottles of soda and ale that were stored there.

Dewey sent the master at arms to arrest the man, but the master returned, saying that he dared not go into the hold since Webster had sworn he would kill anyone who came down.

George Dewey knew that this was the critical moment at which it must be decided whether he, the executive officer, or Webster, the bully, was going to be the master of the crew. With his revolver in hand he started for the hold. As he approached, Webster shouted the threat that had stopped the master at arms, saying that anyone who started down the ladder would be a dead man.

Dewey did not hesitate. He knew that, going down the ladder, his whole body would be exposed before his head would be in a position from which he could see the raging bully below him, yet he went steadily on. As he came to the top of the ladder he called out, "Webster, this is the executive officer, Mr. Dewey. I am coming down, and you may be sure of this: if you raise a finger against me I shall kill you."

Then he scrambled down the ladder as quickly as he could, hoping that it would take Webster a moment to make up his mind what to do, and found the bully standing with a bottle upraised, ready to throw. But as Dewey, his revolver pointed steadily at the man, approached quickly, Webster lowered his arm, dropped the bottle, and submitted quietly to arrest.

This was the beginning of a new era on board the *Colorado*. There were a few more minor incidents before the ringleaders of the insubordinates were made to understand clearly that Commodore Thatcher and Lieutenant Dewey were determined to have a well-ordered, disciplined ship and would take whatever measures were necessary to bring that condition about. Once this was clearly understood the ship's crew began to work as a team and

Thatcher and Dewey knew that they were ready to do their part in the planned assault on Fort Fisher.

As a softening-up process before the actual attack, an old vessel, the *Louisiana*, was filled with gunpowder and disguised as a blockade runner. Under cover of darkness she was run in close to Fort Fisher by Commander Rhind, Dewey's former captain on the *Agawam*. Time fuses were laid to the powder and the skeleton crew then left the ship and returned to their own vessel which waited, with the rest of the fleet, at the mouth of the Cape Fear River.

All through the night of December 23, Dewey and Thatcher stayed on the deck of the *Colorado*, waiting for the explosion. A little before two o'clock in the morning a flash of light was followed by a dull sound like that of thunder and, some time later, by smoke. Apparently the daring trick had been successful.

Actually, as they learned later, it had been about as helpful as a firecracker might have been. Gunners in Fort Fisher later reported that, though they had heard the explosion, they had thought that it must have been the boiler of a blockade runner that had blown up. No effect whatever had been felt by the fort. Perhaps if the *Louisiana* had been run in closer and grounded, the result would have been far different. As it was, the shock of the explosion seems to have been absorbed by the water.

At daylight, not yet knowing how ineffective the explosion had been, the fleet stood in for the inlet that Fort Fisher commanded, as strangely assorted a group of vessels as ever attempted a harmonized action. Yet, in spite of some initial confusion, the vessels finally came into line in the positions assigned to them, and the push toward the fort began.

In this operation the plan of attack was somewhat different from that used at New Orleans and Port Hudson. As each vessel came into position before the fort it dropped anchors from both bow and stern, thus becoming a stationary floating battery. The *New Ironsides*, leading the first division, opened fire at about one in the afternoon. Half an hour later the *Colorado* was engaged. Until 5:30 the cannonading continued, when the flagship signaled, "Retire for the night." The general opinion was that the fort had been effectively silenced, and that the assault by the land forces, planned for the next day, would be a comparatively simple matter. The only casualties had been caused by the explosion of the boiler on the *Mackinaw*, and the bursting of the 100-pounder Parrot rifled guns that were apparently more dangerous to those who used them than they were to the enemy.

That night the transports, bearing the army troops, arrived, and plans proceeded for the attack the following morning. This time the *Colorado*, the *Minnesota*, and the *Wabash*, having found the depth of the water greater than had been expected, approached more closely to the fort and fired shell after shell, along with the rest of the fleet, in such numbers that it seemed as though the fort must have become a mass of rubble. There were long periods when the Confederate guns were silent, and then salvoes from them would pour forth on the Union fleet.

Unexpectedly, a signal from the flagship ordered all of the ships save the *Minnesota* and the *Colorado* to withdraw. These two were ordered to maintain their positions, but to discontinue action. Consequently, as the rest of the fleet passed out of range, the Confederate batteries concentrated on them. The *Colorado's* capstan was shot away, two guns put out of action, one man killed, and five wounded. For the two ships to continue to obey orders meant virtual annihilation, and Commander Thatcher took matters into his own hands. Discarding the idea of withdrawing against orders, he, as senior officer, signaled the *Minnesota* to fire for her own protection, and signaled the flagship his reason for doing so. Then George Dewey ran along the gun deck. The men were angry because of the order not to fire, which he now countermanded.

"Fire," he kept calling to them. "Fire as fast as you can. That's the only way to stop their fire."

The men obeyed with alacrity, and when the signal finally came for the two ships to retire, the Confederate batteries had been silenced. Even though Fisher still remained in the hands of the Confederates the crew felt a sense of victory.

Three weeks later, on the 12th of January, a fleet of forty-eight men-of-war sailed from their base at Beaufort, southwest of Charleston, escorting a number of army transports. That night all the ships anchored twelve miles from Fort Fisher, and the next day men-of-war took up their old positions and began to pound the fort with heavy fire, while the army troops were being put ashore to encamp and wait until the next day for what was to be the final assault.

On the morning of the fourteenth, at nine o'clock, the signal came for the plan to be put into operation. While the army attacked on the land side sixteen hundred sailors and marines were landed from the warships to attack the sea face of the fort. George Dewey asked Commander Thatcher to allow him to lead the quota from the *Colorado*, but the commander refused. Since Thatcher was next in command of the fleet after Porter, he reasoned that if anything happened to the fleet commander, he, Thatcher, would have to take command, and the command of the *Colorado* would fall to George Dewey.

During the landing of the naval troops and the approach of the land forces, the fleet kept firing its heavy guns. The extent of the bombardment may be judged by the fact that in two days over eighteen thousand shells were discharged against Fort Fisher.

During all of that last day of the battle George Dewey and the other officers and men watched the gallant advances of both the land and naval forces, saw them beaten back by musket fire, saw the wounded and killed fall, and the able-bodied reform their ranks and charge again.

In the end it was the army troops who took first the outer defenses, and finally stormed their way into the inner stronghold. It was a little after dark that the last shot was fired from Fort Fisher, and the last naval battle of the Civil War ended.

On April 9, 1865, Lee surrendered to Grant at Appomatox Courthouse, Virginia, and the Civil War was over. By then George Dewey had been transferred to the *Kearsarge* as executive officer. There he had the happy duty of directing the crew as they dressed ship in celebration of the Union victory.

In the same year Lieutenant Dewey was promoted, becoming Lieutenant Commander at the age of twenty-seven. It was almost unprecedented that a man of this age should receive this rank in the Navy. But in four years of war George Dewey had proved his mettle, and especially his ability to handle men.

Chapter 8
Between Two Wars

By sheer chance, George Dewey had no sooner begun his naval career, at the age of twenty-four, than he became involved in some of the most active, most hazardous, and most exciting events of one of the world's bloodiest conflicts. Here he assumed, and discharged with great honor, responsibilities far beyond those usually faced by men of his age. The years of the Civil War constituted one definite period in his life—a period that prepared him to face whatever responsibilities were placed upon him.

With the war over, he entered a period that was to be a long, comparatively quiet, time of life, until the war with Spain, in 1898, once more placed him in the line of battle and made him a national hero. The story of these intervening years can be quickly told.

After an uneventful year on the *Kearsarge*, he became, for a time, executive officer of the *Canandaigua*. When the executive officer of the *Colorado*, on which Dewey had served at Fort Fisher, was transferred, Rear Admiral Goldsborough, who had been superintendent at Annapolis during George Dewey's first year there, got him back onto his old ship, which was about to start on a European cruise. Some time after the battle of Fort Fisher, Commander Thatcher had been removed. Her new commander and executive had not gotten along well and discipline on the ship was again at a low ebb as it had been when Dewey first joined it in 1864.

"Take the *Colorado*," Goldsborough said, "and make a man-of-war of her."

"Thus," Dewey wrote proudly in his autobiography, "from 1862 to 1867, I had been executive officer on no less than nine ships."

Once more the young officer proved his ability to handle men and make a vessel shipshape. Soon the *Colorado* became an example of discipline and order for the whole Navy.

One of George Dewey's proudest moments came to him during the two years' cruise of his vessel in European waters. While the whole squadron was in the harbor of Cherbourg, France, the *Franklin* came in flying the four-starred flag of George's old hero, Admiral Farragut, now sixty-six years old, but—at least in the eyes of his admirer George Dewey—as hale and vigorous as in the days when Dewey had fought under him on the *Mississippi*.

Dewey was overjoyed when he learned that the admiral was coming on board the *Colorado* with his staff. The ship was given an especially thorough cleaning, the men were carefully instructed in the behavior called for when entertaining so distinguished a guest, and the ship's band of thirty-two pieces, reputed to be the best in the

Navy, welcomed the admiral aboard with martial music.

After inspecting every detail aboard the *Colorado*, Farragut turned to Captain Pennock of the *Franklin*, who had come on board with him, and said, "Pennock, I want the *Franklin* to be just like this."

In George Dewey's life there were two men whom he respected more than all others. One was his father and the other was David Farragut. When the admiral expressed this high praise of Dewey's *Colorado* it was as though his father had said to him, "George, you are doing 'the rest' well."

In September, 1867, with the *Colorado* back in the Brooklyn Navy Yard, Dewey was detached and assigned to the Naval Academy at Annapolis to be in charge of all ships stationed there and of the fourth class of midshipmen.

A month later he was married to Susan Goodwin in Portsmouth and took his bride to Annapolis, where they spent three happy years together. Vice Admiral David D. Porter, Farragut's foster brother, and a close friend of George Dewey, was then superintendent, and was fond of social functions, which Dewey and his wife also enjoyed. Indeed one of the officers at the Academy often referred to it as "Porter's Dancing Academy." George Dewey was to remember those three years with his wife at Annapolis as among the happiest of his life.

When he left the naval academy he was given his first command, the *Narragansett*, but after three months aboard her in New York harbor was transferred to the *Supply* for a short European cruise. After his return, he spent a few months at the Boston Navy Yard and then was sent to the naval torpedo station at Newport.

At Newport, on December 23, 1872, his son George Goodwin Dewey was born. Five days later his wife died and Dewey, now thirty-five, was glad to be assigned to sea duty and leave a station that would always be associated with his grief. His infant son was left in the tender care of his wife's father and mother.

He was promoted to commander and once more assigned to the *Narragansett*, which he joined in Panama Bay in the spring of 1873. For two years he commanded the vessel while she cruised the Gulf of California, surveying the coast and making geodetic charts that are still in use. It was while he was on duty that the news of the *Virginius* affair reached him.

This was during what has come to be known as "The Ten Years War" of revolt of the Cuban people against Spanish rule. The ship *Virginius*, fraudulently flying the American flag, carrying arms to the Cubans as well as nine American passengers, was captured off Cuba by the Spaniards and her captain and fifty-two of the crew and passengers were executed.

Only six survived. Their survival was due to another incident which once more proved that between Britain and America "blood is thicker than water." Captain Lambton Lorraine, in command of the British ship *Niobe*, steamed into Santiago. Hearing of the incident, the captain swung his vessel broadside to the town, uncovered his guns, and sent a message posthaste to shore, announcing that unless the rest of the execution orders were rescinded immediately he would shell the city. The Spaniards, having little to fear from the depleted American Navy of that time, nevertheless respected the might of the British at sea and six of the fifty-nine who had entered the harbor on the *Virginius* remained alive.

Nevertheless the incident almost led to the war between the United States and Spain in which Dewey was to play so important a part twenty-five years later. But the matter was finally settled when Spain paid the United States $80,000 indemnity.

Resentment against Spain was so high in the United States at the time that, until the settlement, war seemed inevitable. One day, entering the ward room of the *Narragansett*, Dewey found several of the officers sitting about in various attitudes of despondency. He asked them what was wrong.

"There's going to be war with Spain," one of them answered, "and here we are, stuck on this job, and we'll be out of it."

"On the contrary," Dewey told him, "we shall be very much in it. If war with Spain is declared the *Narragansett* will take Manila."

Today his remark seems to have been almost prophetic, save for one detail, though twenty-five years were to pass before the prophecy came true. The *Narragansett* did not take Manila, for by 1898 she was obsolete, but, as all the world knows, George Dewey and the squadron that he commanded, in co-operation with the Army, did, when war finally came.

In the spring of 1875 Dewey was detached from the *Narragansett* and was able, for the first time in two years, to spend a little time in Portsmouth and rejoice in the healthy happy growth of his small son.

For the next twenty-three years George Dewey held perhaps as wide a variety of posts as any man in the Navy ever has held. For two years he was a lighthouse inspector, with headquarters in Boston, which gave him the opportunity to see his son George from time to time, much to his delight. He was then made naval secretary of the Lighthouse Board with headquarters in Washington.

Dewey had always loved horses and, during his four years as naval secretary, he often rode in Rock Creek Park. Frequently during these rides he met a bearded elderly gentleman, also riding, and they came to exchange greetings, before Dewey, who liked to ride faster than the other, drew ahead of him. One day he asked a friend who the old man was.

"His name is Bancroft," he was told, and Dewey recognized him as the famous historian, former Secretary of the Navy, and the founder of the United States Naval Academy at Annapolis. The next time they met George Dewey introduced himself, saying, "As an officer of the navy who owes so much to the naval academy that you established, I want to thank you."

Among the friends George Dewey made in Washington were William Babcock Hazen, who had been a brigadier general in the Civil War, and his wife Mildred, twenty years her husband's junior. The friendship formed then was to have important results in Dewey's life, as we shall see later.

Following his tour of land duty, Commander Dewey was given several ships in succession. At the age of forty-seven he was again promoted, this time becoming a captain. One of his ships was the old *Pensacola*, which, along with the *Mississippi*, the first ship on which Dewey had served, had been dragged across the mud at the mouth of the Mississippi River preceding the Battle of New Orleans. Now the old vessel was actually obsolete, but still in service, and, because of the fine spirit of her crew, Dewey was always to remember with pride the fact that he had been her captain for a time.

During the summer of 1885, during a cruise of European waters, King Oscar of Sweden came on board the ship. He was given a glass of wine in the cabin, and, while talking with the group of men who were his hosts, he said, "This is the kind of kingdom to have. I would rather command a man-of-war than be king of any country in the world." He turned to Captain Bridgeman of the *Kearsarge*, who was also aboard, and asked, "Wouldn't you, Captain?"

Bridgeman smiled. "I have only tried the man-of-war, your Majesty," he answered.

At Piraeus, Dewey dined with the royal family. As he was leaving, the king said to him, "The next time you come I hope you will be an admiral." Dewey always regretted that he found it impossible, on his return from Manila after having received the rank of admiral, to again call on the King of Greece to tell him that his hope had been realized.

Dewey's trip home on the *Pensacola* in 1889 was his last experience with a ship under sail and, for that matter, his last tour of duty at sea until after he had been made a commodore in 1896.

In Washington he found that his old friend Brigadier General William Babcock Hazen had died. But Dewey's friendship with his widow, Mildred, continued.

Now he served in a succession of capacities on shore duty. For a time he was chief of the Bureau of Equipment of the Navy Department, then a member of the Lighthouse Board, and later president of the Board of Inspection and Survey.

Long before he had achieved these positions he, along with other of the more progressive officers of the Navy, had been deeply concerned because the United States seemed completely uninterested in the fact that the old, outmoded ships of its Navy were, in a sense, the laughing stock of the world. There was not another major power that was not better equipped with armored fighting ships and long-range guns that could have brought about a major catastrophe for America had we been forced to go to war with any of them.

Actually this was a reflection of what, up to that time, had always been the American attitude toward its armed forces. We had been a little like the man who, when asked why he did not mend the large leaks in the roof of his house, answered, "When it isn't raining there's no need to mend it, and when it is raining it's too uncomfortable to work outside." Why, America seemed to ask, do we need a navy or an army when we are not at war?

It was only because the South was more poorly equipped with warships than we at the outbreak of the Civil War, and because the North had greater resources with which to build new ships, that the Union was able to win its naval battles. By the time Lee surrendered at Appomatox, the Union Navy had become the largest in number of ships and manpower in the world.

But, with the war over, while other nations continued in technical progress and ship construction, we relaxed, letting our monitors rust at anchor. While other nations brought out new and improved ironclads, we kept repairing our old vessels and using them as long as they would hold together.

But during the late eighties and early nineties, partly, perhaps, because of the increasing tension between Spain and America, the United States began to build a new navy. It was the responsibility of the Board of Inspection of the Navy to see that the construction of all the ships built under the new program was sound, and, after trials, to accept or reject every ship after it was finished.

Thus, as president of the board, George Dewey presided at the trials of the *Texas, Maine, Iowa, Indiana,* and *Massachusetts.* There were other ships also built during his period as president of the board, and approved by him, but these five are of especial interest because four of them comprised the major part of the squadron that demolished the Spanish squadron at Santiago, while another group of five ships under George Dewey was busy destroying another Spanish squadron in Manila Bay. The *Maine*, as all the world knows, played another role in the history of our war with Spain.

His son, George Goodwin Dewey, had entered Princeton University in the fall of 1892. During the years in which the elder Dewey had been at sea, father and son had seen so little of each other that the boy would hardly have recognized his father had they met unexpectedly on the street. His father was not an eloquent man, nor one who showed his gentler emotions easily, and in his autobiography he is reticent about his son.

But it is known from other sources that during young George's years at Princeton he received the princely allowance of $1,500 a year from his father, plus extras in times of need, that young George sometimes visited his father in Washington, and that when the boy was invited to become a member of the Cottage Club—one of the four most important social organizations at the university—his father went to Princeton to celebrate with him. Apparently, though the two had a dignified and somewhat aloof respect and affection for each other, they never achieved the close companionship that more fortunate fathers and sons, who are able to be with each other more, sometimes manage.

One amusing story has been told by the son, which indicates that perhaps they did understand each other well enough to depend upon each other, and also that the elder Dewey enjoyed making an impression on young ladies, and sometimes may have attempted to seem younger than his years.

In the summer of 1893 Captain Dewey, as a member of the Lighthouse Board, made an inspection cruise aboard the *America*. While the ship was at Martha's Vineyard, its skipper, Captain Wright, went ashore to get Dewey's son who was going to spend the night aboard. While the skipper was gone, two young girls in a rowboat came alongside the vessel and wanted to inspect it.

George Dewey himself became their guide and obviously enjoyed himself hugely. The girls were still on board when Goodwin Dewey returned. Dewey introduced the girls to Captain Wright, then, turning to his son, he said, "And this is my younger brother." At 56 he apparently was unwilling to let two pretty girls know that he was old enough to have a son of college age.

Chapter 9
First Steps on the Road to Manila Bay

The tension between Spain and the United States had not ended with the settlement of the *Virginius* affair in 1873, nor had it actually begun at that time. There was provocation on both sides. Actually ever since Thomas Jefferson had been President, the United States had seriously considered acquiring Cuba—by purchase if possible, or by conquest if it turned out to be not for sale. Spanish resentment of this attitude was not unnatural.

Throughout the years Cuba, lying so close to the shores of the United States, had been a problem to American statesmen. In 1825 President Fillmore had refused to join Great Britain and France in guaranteeing Spanish authority in the islands. In 1854 the Ostend Manifesto, written largely by James Buchanan, urged the United States to acquire Cuba either by purchase or conquest. When President Grant offered to buy the islands from Spain, the latter refused to sell them.

Lying on the other side of the world was another possession of the Spaniards, the Philippine Islands, taken during the Spanish Conquest in 1564, and, like Cuba, in revolt against Spanish rule during the nineteenth century.

In 1895 when a new Cuban rebellion broke out, the American Navy found its task of maintaining neutrality a difficult one. As in the 1960's when many Cubans fled the dictatorial rule of Fidel Castro and came to the United States so, in the 1890's did many come to America, achieve American citizenship, and then return to Cuba to fight against the power of Spain. In these attempts they often had the aid of sympathetic Americans. Generally speaking, our "neutrality" was what might have been called a "neutrality against Spain." Month by month the danger of war seemed to increase.

Everyone knew that, if war came, it would be a war in which naval action would be of the greatest importance, and that the sea battles would be fought not only in the Caribbean, in the vicinity of Cuba, but also in the Pacific where a Spanish squadron was stationed as a part of the power by which Spain held the Philippines.

In 1897 the question arose of a successor to the sixty-two-year-old Acting Rear Admiral McNair in command of the Asiatic Squadron, and about to retire. Obviously the choice of the man at this time was a matter of more than ordinary importance. If war with Spain came, the man in command of our warships in Asiatic waters would be bound to play an important part in it.

Dewey, now fifty-nine years old, had always been especially interested in the Philippines, and had read everything he could about the islands. He knew that he, now a commodore, was being considered for the post, but he knew that Commodore John A. Howell was also being considered. Howell, who had been a classmate of Dewey's at Annapolis, was in command of an antiquated fleet protecting the Atlantic Coast, from Virginia to Maine, against a possible surprise attack by a Spanish fleet. Dewey knew that Rear Admiral A. S. Crowninshield, chief of the Bureau of Navigation and a close advisor of Secretary of the Navy Long, would favor Howell over himself.

But there was another man who had an especial interest in the matter—Assistant Secretary of the Navy Theodore Roosevelt. And Theodore Roosevelt had a great deal of confidence in George Dewey.

Roosevelt's interest in Dewey had become aroused several years earlier at a time when it seemed as though we might become involved in war with Chile. At the time Dewey was head of the Bureau of Equipment.

In 1891 a rebellion in Chile attacked the authority of the president, Don José Manuel Balmaceda. United States President Benjamin Harrison and his Secretary of State James G. Blaine continued to recognize and support the Balmaceda government, thus antagonizing the rebels. In May of that year the ship *Itata* entered San Diego harbor in an attempt to take a cargo of arms to the Chilean insurgents. President Harrison immediately ordered the ship seized and held in quarantine, which was done, but the Chilean crew overpowered the Americans and at once put out to sea, taking two U.S. Marshals with them. Later the ship was surrendered to an American squadron, only to be returned to Chile after an American court had decided that the United States had had no right to hold her in the first place.

But the incident had not unnaturally strained relations between the United States and Chile still more. In October the strain was increased almost to the breaking point when a group of unarmed sailors, ashore at Valparaiso from the *U.S.S. Baltimore* got into a saloon brawl with a group of patriotic Chileans. When fifty armed Chilean policemen joined the fight, two of the Americans were killed, and nearly twenty wounded. Those who were not taken to the morgue or a hospital were taken to jail.

During the next few weeks all Americans thought that any day might bring a declaration of war against Chile. Two United States warships lay in the waters off Argentina. Obviously, in case of war, they would be ordered to proceed at once from the Atlantic, around Cape Horn into the Pacific, to join in the conflict against Chile. But in order to be able to do this they would need coal. Yet, if the war did not occur, and the coal had been bought, it would not be needed.

Theodore Roosevelt told in his autobiography, in 1920, that "Dewey purchased the coal and was ready to move at once if need arose." A lesser man, Roosevelt thought, would have referred the matter to a higher authority, thus inevitably losing precious time. "In a crisis the man worth his salt is the man who meets the needs of the situation in whatever way is necessary. The affair blew over; the need to move did not occur; and for some time there seemed to be a chance that Dewey would get into

Theodore Roosevelt

trouble over having purchased the coal without orders from his superiors. . . However the people higher up ultimately stood by Dewey."

Apparently this episode greatly increased Theodore Roosevelt's respect for Dewey, and by the time eventual conflict with Spain seemed inevitable, the two men were close friends. In many ways they were alike—especially in a certain boldness, a belief in offense as the best defense, and a willingness to take responsibility by making quick and independent decisions and acting on them, one of the traits that Dewey admired most of all in his hero David Farragut.

Roosevelt showed clearly why he was in favor of appointing Dewey to replace the retiring McNair in an article in *McClure's* Magazine, October, 1899. He wrote of "the high professional reputation" that was Dewey's, "and the character he had established for willingness to accept responsibility, for sound judgment, and for utter fearlessness. Probably the best way (although no way is infallible) to tell the worth of a naval commander as yet untried in war is to get at the estimate in which he is held by the best fighting men who would have to serve under him. In the summer of 1897 there were, in Washington, captains and commanders who later won honor for themselves and their country in the war with Spain, and who were already known for the dash and skill with which they handled their ships, the excellence of their gun practice, the good discipline of their crews, and their eager desire to win honorable renown. All these men were a unit in their faith in Commodore Dewey, in their desire to serve under him, should the chance arise, and in their unquestioning belief that he was the man to meet an emergency in a way that would do credit to the flag."

There was no question that Roosevelt favored Dewey, no question either that Dewey wanted the post. But Roosevelt had been given to understand that Howell would be given the appointment. However it was not like Theodore Roosevelt to give up a plan that he thought was in the best interests of the country. He knew that political pressure from a high source had been used to influence Secretary Long to appoint Howell. The thing to do, he reasoned, was to fight fire with fire. He called Dewey to him.

Dewey himself tells the story of that meeting in his autobiography:

" 'I want you to go,' Mr. Roosevelt declared. 'You are the man who will be equal to the emergency if one arises. Do you know any senators?'

"My heart was set on having the Asiatic Squadron. It seemed to me that we were inevitably drifting into war with Spain. In command of an efficient force in the Far East, with a free hand to act in consequence of being so far away from Washington, I could strike promptly and successfully at the Spanish force in the Philippines.

" 'Senator Proctor is from my state,' I said to Mr. Roosevelt. 'He is an old friend of the family and my father was of service to him when he was a young man.'

" 'You could not have a better sponsor,' Mr. Roosevelt exclaimed. 'Lose no time in having him speak a word for you.' "

The matter was quickly accomplished. On the very day that Roosevelt spoke to Dewey, Dewey spoke to Proctor, and Proctor to President McKinley, who promised to see to it at once that Dewey received the appointment.

A few days later Dewey was told that Secretary Long was indignant with him for having used political influence. He went immediately to the Secretary.

"I understand," he said, "that you are displeased with me for having used influence to secure command of the Asiatic Squadron. I did so because it was the only way of offsetting influence that was being used on another officer's behalf."

Secretary Long stiffly denied that any such influence had been used on behalf of anyone else, and Dewey left him. A few hours later, however, he received what amounted to an apology from Secretary Long, though the cool tone of the note showed that the secretary was still displeased. In the note Long reported that he had just learned that a letter from an influential person supporting Howell's candidacy had come during his absence from the office and he had only now seen it.

On October 21, 1897, Dewey was summoned to Secretary Long's office and was handed the following order:

Commodore George Dewey, U. S. N.
President, Board of Inspection and Survey,
Navy Department, Washington, D. C.

Sir:

On November 30th, 1897, you will regard your-
self detached from duty as president of the Board of
Inspection and Survey, Navy Department, Washington, D. C., and from such other duty as may
have been assigned you, you will proceed to San
Francisco, Cal., and thence to Yokohama, Japan,
taking passage in the steamer of the Pacific Mail
Steamship Company, sailing from San Francisco on
December 7th next. Upon your arrival at Yokohama
you will report to Rear Admiral Frederick V. Mc-
Nair, U. S. N., the Commander-in-chief of the
Asiatic Station, aboard the U. S. F. S. *Olympia*, for
duty as Commander-in-chief of that station, as the
relief of that officer

Respectfully
John D. Long
Secretary

Dewey was elated. But one element in the situation
was a deep and bitter disappointment to him. He was to
retain the rank of Commodore. In 1853 when Commodore
Matthew Galbraith Perry had made his famous visit to
Japan, no rank of Rear Admiral existed in the U. S. Navy.
But ever since that time every commander of the Asiatic
Squadron had either the rank of Rear Admiral, or, if all of
the six posts of that rank allowed in the Navy were full, of

Acting Rear Admiral. Going to the Pacific in his capacity of squadron commander, but with the rank of Commodore, would place him lower in rank than the commanders of practically all of the foreign fleets with which he would come into contact. George Dewey, his son George Goodwin Dewey, and Theodore Roosevelt, all have attributed the fact that he was not given the rank of Acting Rear Admiral to Secretary Long's dislike of him, the secretary's desire to appoint Howell instead, and his anger at Dewey's having exerted political pressure through Senator Proctor and President McKinley.

Secretary Long, however, has reported quite a different version of the story. In his authoritative book, *The New American Navy*, published in 1903, he wrote:

"The Asiatic Squadron, in case of war with Spain offered the larger probable opportunity for distinction, although the European Squadron was a choice flag command of the Navy and included Spanish waters. I decided to give Dewey the Asiatic and Howell the European station, and this arrangement, on my submitting it to President McKinley, who had made no suggestion in the matter and who always left such matters to the Secretary, was approved by him. I remember his simply saying to me, in his characteristically pleasant way, 'Are you satisfied that Dewey is a good man for the place and that his head is level?', to which I affirmatively answered. Political or personal influence had nothing to do with his selection, which was entirely my own."

There was some opposition to Dewey's appointment from certain congressmen who had wanted to see it given to friends of theirs, and here and there such epithets as "Commodore ahorseback" and "Dewey the Dude" were heard, but the appointment, once made, remained firm.

During the five weeks left to George Dewey in Washington he was busy clearing up his affairs in the Bureau of Inspection and Survey to turn over to his successor, arranging personal matters for an absence of two years, learning as much about the Philippines as he could, buying every book that he could find on the subject, and learning all that he could about the condition of the Asiatic Squadron.

Learning that the squadron did not have even its normal peacetime allotment of ammunition, he set about correcting the situation. The Navy Department told him that, though it had been planning to replenish the supply, the trans-Pacific commercial steamers refused to carry it, and shipment of it would have to await the sailing of the U. S. S. *Charleston*, which was under repair and would probably not be ready for sea for six months.

This was far from good enough for George Dewey. Gaining the vigorous and influential support of his friend, Assistant Secretary of the Navy Roosevelt, the Commodore finally succeeded in having an order issued that the *Concord*, then being fitted for Asiatic duty at the Mare Island Navy Yard off Vallejo, California, should carry as much ammunition as her limited capacity would permit.

In San Francisco, Dewey pointed out to the commandant of the Mare yard the importance of putting on board every possible pound of ammunition, and suggested that by stopping for supplies at Honolulu, and buying in Japan other things which ordinarily would be carried from the United States, much more valuable space could be made available for this essential cargo.

Both the commandant and Commander Asa Walker of the *Concord* were fully co-operative and, as a result, a small vessel of only seventeen hundred tons displacement carried nearly thirty-five tons of ammunition.

But Dewey knew that he dare not wait six months for the *Charleston* for more ammunition. So he arranged that about thirty-seven tons be shipped to Honolulu by the old sloop of war *Mohican,* to be transferred there to the cruiser *Baltimore* which, as tension mounted, would undoubtedly be sent to reinforce the Asiatic Squadron.

Thus, when Dewey sailed out of San Francisco harbor, he knew that a dangerous shortage had been at least partially corrected.

Chapter 10
The Commodore Takes Command

After a voyage of what was actually sixteen days, but which became seventeen by the calendar, "because," as Dewey wrote to his son George the next day, "we dropped a day when we crossed the 180 degrees of longitude," Commodore Dewey stretched his legs briefly in Yokohama on Christmas Day, 1897, where the Pacific mail steamer *Gaelic* made an overnight stop. In the letter to his son he added, "I am sixty years old today and you were twenty-five on the twenty-third. We are getting on!"

Then he continued with the *Gaelic* to Nagasaki where the *Olympia*, which was to be his flagship, awaited him. As he approached the *Olympia* he saw with deep satisfaction her sleek fine lines, typical of the new Navy, which had at last recognized that steam was the power of the day and of the future. The *Olympia* had two towering masts, but no sails. A gun turret was mounted at the bow, and another at the stern. Each carried two 8-inch rifled cannons, capable of firing accurately at long range. The ship also had ten 5-inch rapid-fire guns, fourteen 6-

pounders, seven 1-pounders, and six Whitehead torpedo tubes. Her graceful bow slanted backwards from the waterline.

The Commodore felt a happy excitement mounting in him when he boarded the *Olympia* on January 1. He thought of her mass of 5,870 tons, her two engines, which gave her the speed of over twenty-one knots (exceptional at that time), and her decks, protected by four-inch armor. He knew that he was about to take over the best-protected cruiser in the U. S. Navy. He would also have under his command the *Baltimore*, *Boston*, and *Raleigh*, of the same general type as the *Olympia*, but less powerful, as well as the gunboats *Concord* and *Petrel*, and a monitor, *Monocacy*, an obsolete paddle-wheel steamer of the Civil War period.

Rear Admiral McNair received him aboard the flagship, and together the two officers examined the squadron records and inspected the ship. Dewey rested the next day, and studied the ship's documents. On Monday, January 3, 1898, the Commodore took command of the ship in an impressive ceremony. The crew and officers, in their dress uniforms, stood at attention while Admiral McNair and his staff marched aft to face the flag. There they were joined by Commodore Dewey, his flag lieutenant T. S. Brumby, his flag secretary Ensign H. H. Caldwell, and his aide, F. B. Upham. After a brief address in which Admiral McNair thanked his officers and men for their co-operation, and reported to his successor, with some little pride, that his squadron was in first-class shape, he gave his last order on board the *Olympia*, telling the flagship's captain, Charles V. Gridley, to haul down the Admiral's two-starred flag. A thirteen-gun salute was given to the retiring Admiral, and the flag came down.

Commodore Dewey then approached Admiral Mc-Nair and saluted. Returning the salute briskly, the Admiral turned and joined his staff. Dewey then gave his first command on the *Olympia*, ordering Captain Gridley to raise his Commodore's pennant. It was done, and as the broad blue flag reached the top of the mast, the Commodore's eleven-gun salute was fired in honor of the new flag officer.

Few persons—with the probable exception of Theodore Roosevelt, Commodore Dewey, and Senator Lodge—foresaw the battle that was to make Dewey famous. The Asiatic Squadron was not in the East in preparation for war with Spain, but rather to keep an eye on the Chinese situation. It was at a time when the great powers of Europe were in conflict over the division of spoils in China, and our ships were there to protect United States citizens in the Orient.

But it is reasonable to believe that in the mind of the fighter, George Dewey, there was even something like hope that the war which seemed probable with Spain would begin soon, and that he would be able to distinguish himself in it. Only a few months earlier, thinking regretfully of his approaching retirement, he had said to a friend in Montpelier, "I don't want war, but without it there is little opportunity for a naval man to distinguish himself. There will be no war before I retire . . . and I will be

Dewey's flagship, the "Olympia" (sketched from the ship itself, now a museum at Philadelphia)

known in history . . . as George Dewey who . . . retired as Rear Admiral at the age limit." Actually, of
course, as he took command of the *Olympia*, he was
merely a commodore. How near he was to the event
which would give him a rank higher than that, and write
his name large on the pages of history, not even he could
have foreseen.

It is interesting, in the light of what was to happen so
soon, that Admiral McNair's letter of transmittal, with
which he turned over the ship's records to Dewey, made
only one minor reference to the Philippines. It mentioned
the fact that newspaper accounts reported that the native
population was in rebellion against Spanish rule, but said
that there was no information to show that American interests were in any way affected.

The statement was a reflection of the general attitude
in the United States. Americans were in an aggressive
mood and almost eager for the war with Spain which
almost everyone, by now, had come to believe was inevitable. But most of them thought of it only in terms of an
American attack on Cuba, and the possibility of Spanish
attacks along the Atlantic coast. Many of them would not
have been able to tell you where the Philippines were. No
American naval vessel had been there for years, and during Dewey's search in Washington for information he
had found that the latest report on the islands in the Office
of Naval Intelligence had been made in 1876.

Charles B. Harris was at that time consul at Nagasaki.
Dewey has told in his autobiography how Mrs. Harris, a

strong advocate for peace and interested in foreign missions, asked him why America needed to maintain an expensive navy. "I laughingly told her," he reported, "that sometimes missionaries found their lives in danger and asked for protection. . . . After the battle, in answer to Mr. Harris's letter of congratulations, I said that I trusted that Mrs. Harris now knew why we maintained a navy, to which he replied that not only did she know, but so did more than eighty million other Americans."

After Perry's visit to Japan in 1853, it had become the custom for each new commander in chief of our Asiatic Squadron to ask for an audience with the Emperor of Japan, but the custom had been neglected for some time before Dewey's arrival in the East. This seeming discourtesy had offended the sensitive Japanese Court. The conscientious George Dewey, however, feeling that a part of his duty was to further friendly relations with Japan, immediately requested the privilege of a visit to court and, having received a courteous invitation, sailed around the southern tip of the island of Kyushu and along the eastern coast of Honshu to Yokohama, where he was expecting daily the arrival of the *Concord* with the ammunition that his squadron would so desperately need in case of war. From there he went by train to Tokyo, where both the Emperor and Empress received him with the greatest honors and courtesy. "What a contrast," he wrote later, "was my reception to that of the other American commodore [Perry] who had cast anchor in the Gulf of Yeddo forty-four years previously!"

As a result of the friendliness established by that visit Dewey was later to report with the greatest appreciation the courtesies shown him by the Japanese Navy in Manila Bay, where there was always one or more Japanese vessels during the time when he maintained a blockade after his destruction of the Spanish fleet. Thus another of history's remarkable contrasts is evident, when we think of this, and of our bitter fighting with the Japanese in the Philippines during World War II!

On February 9 the *Concord* reached Yokohama, and transferred her ammunition the next day. She had brought all that she could carry, but not enough to fill the ammunition storage compartments of Dewey's squadron, and he felt some apprehension. But there was nothing he could do about it now, and so, on his own initiative, he took the next step toward what he was convinced was to be the role his squadron would be called upon to play.

He had already ordered the *Petrel* to Hong Kong, which was much closer to the Philippines than was Yokahama. On the 11th he sailed in the *Olympia* for the same port. There he found news waiting for him. The *Maine* had been sunk in Havana harbor! The next day the news was confirmed by the following cable:

> Dewey, Hong Kong:
> Maine destroyed at Havana February 15th by accident. The President directs all colors to be half masted until further orders. Inform vessels under your command by telegraph.
>
> Long.

It remained for the aggressive Assistant Secretary of the Navy, Theodore Roosevelt, to send somewhat more realistic orders on a day when his superior, Secretary Long, was absent from the office. On February 25 he cabled:

> Dewey, Hong Kong:
> Order the squadron except the *Monocacy* to Hong Kong. Keep full of coal. In the event of declaration of war Spain your duty will be to see that the Spanish Squadron does not leave the Asiatic coast, and then offensive operations in Philippine Islands
> . . .
>
> Roosevelt.

The message was evidence of the difference in temperaments between Secretary of the Navy Long and his assistant. When Long learned of Roosevelt's cable, he wrote in his diary, "The very devil seemed to possess him. Yesterday afternoon he has gone at things like a bull in a China shop. It shows how the best fellow in the world and with splendid capabilities is worse than no use if he lacks a cool head and careful discretion."

But regardless of the attitudes of President McKinley and his Secretary of the Navy, Theodore Roosevelt and George Dewey knew that the long-expected war with Spain could not now be far off.

Chapter 11
"Remember the Maine"

In January, 1898, the *Maine*, one of the Navy's first two modern battleships, was stationed off Key West, Florida, under the command of Captain Charles D. Sigsbee. The *Maine*, known as "Armored Cruiser No. 1," was a vessel of 6,600 tons, carrying 10- and 6-inch guns, with 11-inch armor. Her vertical engines, more efficient than the old horizontal engines, furnished 9,000 horsepower. She quickly became the pride of America.

On January 12, rioting, led by Spanish officers, broke out in Havana, in protest against a proposed new constitution. Along with the demonstrations, threats were made against American citizens. Fitzhugh Lee, Consul General at Havana, cabled Washington, asking that the *Maine* be sent if Blanco, the military commander, failed to keep order. On January 24, Lee received a cable saying that the *Maine* had been ordered to Cuba. The vessel entered Havana harbor on the twenty-fifth, and Captain Sigsbee paid courtesies to the Spanish authorities and the people in an attempt to convince them that America was friendly.

In a number of ways the Spanish authorities returned

the courtesies, but with a certain amount of coolness that was significant of the feeling of tension that existed. When Sigsbee attended a bullfight with his officers, someone thrust into his hand a pamphlet condemning "the Yankee pigs" for sending a warship to Cuba and calling on all loyal sons of Spain to throw the pigs out! And written in English, at the bottom of the copy handed to Sigsbee, was "Look out for your ship!" At the same time a large billboard in the city bore a cartoon showing a Cuban loyalist putting a banana peel under the foot of a figure plainly intended to depict Uncle Sam.

The tension mounted rapidly to its climax after that. When the "Yankee Pigs" pamphlet was published in American newspapers, the voice of the American public was loud in its wrath. On February 8, feeling was further inflamed by the publication of a letter from the Spanish Ambassador to Washington, Senor Dupuy de Lome, written to a friend in Havana, stolen in Cuba, and sent to America. In it the senor gave evidence of Spanish treachery in its relations with the United States, and called President McKinley "weak, a caterer to the rabble, and a cheap politician who wishes to . . . stand well with the jingoes of his party." Even though Spain apologized and recalled de Lome, American feeling reached a high point of frenzy.

President McKinley, however, still sought to avoid war, and the de Lome episode might have been forgotten had it not been for what happened a little before ten o'clock on the evening of February 15.

Captain Sigsbee was in his cabin on the *Maine*, writing a report, when a tremendous explosion in the forward part of the vessel rocked the ship, and was instantly followed by a second. All the lights were extinguished, and the ship began to sink rapidly. All but two of the lifeboats had been made unusable. Boats from the steamer *City of Washington* and the Spanish cruiser *Alfonso XIII* rushed to the aid of those still living aboard the *Maine*.

Captain Sigsbee was one of those who made his way safely to shore and immediately cabled the Secretary of the Navy:

> *Maine* blown up in Havana Harbor at 9:40 tonight and destroyed. Many wounded and doubtless more killed or drowned. Wounded and others on board Spanish man-of-war and Ward Liner. Send lighthouse keepers from Key West for crew and a few pieces of equipment above. No one has clothing other than that upon him. Public opinion should be suspended until after further report. All officers believed to be saved. Jenkins and Merritt not yet accounted for. Many Spanish officers, including General Blanco, now with me to express sympathy.

Both the U. S. Secretary of the Navy and the Spanish government set up inquiries to determine the cause of the explosions. Both sent divers down to examine the hulk, the Americans carrying on their investigation inside and outside the ship, the Spaniards (because they were not permitted to go inside) only on the outside. The American report expressed the opinion that the explosion had been

The "Maine"

caused by a submarine mine, but made no attempt to judge who had placed it. The Spanish investigators decided there had been an internal explosion in the forward magazine.

To this day no one actually knows what the cause was, and doubtless no one ever will, for after another investigation, in 1911, which resulted in no firm conclusion, what remained of the *Maine* was towed out to deep water and sunk.

But in the minds of a large proportion of the American public, already inflamed with antagonism against Spain, there was no doubt. On the 16th there appeared in the American newspapers headlines such as this from the Boston *Herald*:

TWO OFFICERS AND 251 MEN

APPALLING DEATH ROLL CAUSED BY THE BATTLESHIP MAINE EXPLOSION

CAUSE OF THE DISASTER STILL REMAINS A MYSTERY

Actually the official count later reported that 260 men had lost their lives in the explosion or by drowning.

But calling it "a mystery" and cautioning Americans to withhold judgment had little effect. The American people's wrath descended on the Spaniards. No one knows who first said it, but anyone living today who was over seven years old in 1898 remembers how the slogan "Remember the Maine! To Hell with Spain!" swept across the country. The clamor for war increased.

Meanwhile Dewey with his squadron (minus the *Monocacy,* which was laid up at Shanghai) waited at Hong Kong for further orders. But he did not wait in idleness. Every ship in the squadron was thoroughly overhauled and kept constantly filled with coal and provisions, ready to move at a moment's notice. The crew were given intensive drill, the machinery put into prime condition, and preparations made to put ashore all superfluous material and woodwork, to give the men more room for action and to reduce the fire hazard.

Later he was to say "the Battle of Manila Bay was won in Hong Kong harbor," meaning, of course, that the intensive discipline the men received there was what made the victory possible.

It was a trying time in international relations in the Far East, and the harbor was crowned with men-of-war from several nations, among them a German squadron under the command of Prince Henry of Prussia. Dewey was not aware that the Prince had sent a cable to the Kaiser saying that "the Philippines have decided upon revolt against Spain, and would gladly place themselves under the protection of a European power, especially Germany." Later, the German desire to take over the Philippines accounted for the petty annoyances that Dewey was to suffer at the hands of the German squadron in Manila Bay after the battle.

But during the stay in Hong Kong harbor the most cordial relations existed between the German and American officers and crews. From this fact arose a strange little incident of the sort which often gives rise to difficult international relations. Commodore Dewey handled it with dignity, but in such a way that what might have been a serious matter became a minor unpleasant incident.

When a group of German seamen came aboard the *Olympia* on a visit, the officer of the deck and several members of the crew of the *Olympia* recognized one of them, a member of the crew of the cruiser *Gefion*, as a deserter from an American ship. Since he wore the German uniform and belonged to the personnel of a German man-of-war he could not be arrested, but Dewey ordered him to leave the ship immediately. Later the Commodore wrote to the rear admiral in command of the German squadron, and asked for the man's surrender as a deserter, but when the German officer refused on the grounds that he was both a German subject and a seaman in the German Navy, the matter was dropped.

Another guest aboard the *Olympia* (though he did not arrive until after the squadron had left Hong Kong) was much more welcome. The American consul at Manila, Mr. O. F. Williams, had stuck to his post in spite of threats, warnings that his life was in danger, and notification from the Governor-General of the Philippines that the government could no longer be responsible for his safety. Only when Dewey sent an urgent request for him to join the squadron did he leave. Meanwhile Williams' cables and letters brought much valuable information. He reported, for instance, that six new guns had been mounted on Corregidor at the entrance to Manila Bay, and gave an account of the number of Spanish warships in the bay, of the feverish work being carried on to strengthen the fortifications, and of the rumors that continually were passed about in the streets of the city. One was that an attack by the American Navy was imminent, another that a coalition of all the European nations was being formed against the United States. But perhaps the wildest of all was the story that the United States had become so frightened by the prospect of war that our government had begged the Pope to intercede with Spain in order to save us from destruction by the Spanish Army and Navy. This one, Williams reported, was considered so authentic that the government had ordered it proclaimed in all of the Philippine churches!

On March 31 Dewey wrote to Secretary Long repeating the information he had received from Williams and other sources, giving an account of the excellent condition and preparation for war of his squadron, and adding:

"I believe I am not overconfident in stating that, with the squadron now under my command the (Spanish) vessels could be taken and the defenses of Manila reduced in one day. There is every reason to believe that with Manila taken or even blockaded, the rest of the islands would fall either to the insurgents or to ourselves, as they are only held through the support of the navy and are dependent upon Manila for supplies. Information has just reached me that there are 5,000 armed rebels in camp near Manila . . . willing to assist us."

He expressed the same confidence in a letter written to his son a few days later. It is an especially interesting letter: it shows that though confident he was well aware of the danger to himself; and also that in the midst of his tensions and his extreme busyness, he could still think of small everyday, practical things.

"The news today is decidedly warlike, and I have made my arrangements for a descent on Manila as soon as war is declared . . . I wish you would send me six cases of Whitteman Bros. and Co. shoe polish for patent leather shoes . . .

"Another thing, in case anything should happen to me during the war, you will become my sole heir to between $80,000 and $90,000. I wish you to pay your Aunt Mary Greeley during her life the sum of five hundred dollars a year, $500 . . .

"I have written the Dept. that I expect to capture the Spanish ships and reduce the defenses of Manila in one day. With much love,

Your affectionate father,
George Dewey.

P.S. The polish comes in small round boxes and is a paste."

To his sister he wrote in the same confident vein, predicting the destruction of the Spanish squadron and defenses in one day, but made no mention of the possibility of his own death.

European efforts were made to prevent the war. Six European powers framed a note to President McKinley, expressing the hope that "for humanity's sake you will not go to war." McKinley answered, "We hope that if we do

President William McKinley

go to war you will understand that it is for humanity's sake."

On April 11 the President asked from Congress, and received, the power to use the military and naval forces of the United States, if necessary, to end the hostilities between Spain and the people of Cuba.

Dewey found later that, in spite of Mr. Williams' care, he had underestimated the defenses of Manila. He had failed, for instance, to learn of twenty-odd small gunboats in Philippine waters, of seventeen heavy rifled guns at the mouth of the bay, and of forty other guns mounted in the Manila and Cavite fortifications.

Meanwhile the Commodore was cheered by arrangements for coal and other provisions from Chinese sources that the commander of the *Monocacy*, stationed at Shanghai, made, and by a cable from Secretary Long saying that the *Baltimore* was bringing more ammunition and would join the Asiatic Squadron.

One of the odd aspects of the situation at this time is that, although the Spanish naval officers (as was revealed later) foresaw disaster for their squadron at Manila in case of an engagement, other Europeans believed that the American Asiatic Squadron was doomed to destruction. Dewey tells in his autobiography how, "after our officers had been entertained at dinner at the Hong Kong Club by a British Regiment, the universal remark among our hosts was, 'a fine set of fellows, but unhappily we shall never see them again.' "

During the last week in Hong Kong practically every day brought a new development. On the 17th of March the *McCulloch* (a revenue steamer that had been at Singapore on the way to San Francisco) arrived to join the squadron. On board were two newspaper correspondents. One was Edward W. Harden of the *New York World*. The other was the 28-year-old John T. McCutcheon, then a correspondent for the *Chicago Record*, but later to become better known as the famous cartoonist of the *Chicago Tribune*.

Earlier, J. L. Stickney, who had been graduated from Annapolis but later had resigned to enter journalism, had arrived from Hong Kong and asked permission to accompany the Commodore on the flagship. He was then a correspondent for the *New York Herald*. Dewey welcomed him, and, because the *Olympia* was shorthanded for junior officers, and Stickney had had naval training, made him his volunteer aide. These three men formed the core of a group of newspapermen who later reported the Battle of Manila Bay and became friends and admirers of Dewey. After the battle, Stickney wrote a biography of the Commodore who, by then, was an admiral.

On the 19th the ships were painted gray in preparation for war. Another two days passed and Dewey received a cable saying that the Atlantic Squadron was blockading Cuba, and that though war had not yet been declared, it might be at any moment. The following day, the 22nd, Dewey greeted with delight the sight of the *Baltimore* steaming into the harbor, while in the Atlantic the U. S. cruiser *Nashville* captured the first prize of war, the Spanish ship *Buena Ventura*. On the 23rd, the Commodore received a letter from the acting Governor of Hong Kong, Major-General Black, saying that, because of Great Britain's neutrality the American squadron must leave the harbor not later than 4 P. M. on April 25.

Then came a minor irritant that Dewey ironed out with his customary ingenuity and that readiness to make independent decisions which had won Theodore Roosevelt's admiration. Commander B. P. Lamberton arrived on a Pacific mail steamer. He was under orders from the Navy Department to take command of the *Boston*. But Captain Frank Wildes, then in charge of the ship, refused to step down without making a protest to Washington. Commodore Dewey, recognizing the urgency of the situation, and the value of efficient and speedy preparation, knew that there was no time for personal squabbles or long exchanges of cables with Washington, so he solved the problem by taking Lamberton on his flagship and making him chief of staff. "Thus," he recalled in his autobiography, "I secured the aid of a most active and accomplished officer at a time when there was positive need of his services; but not until later did I realize how much I owed to the sympathetic companionship of Lamberton's sunny, hopeful, and tactful disposition."

On the 24th, one day before the deadline set by the British, the *Boston, Concord, Petrel, McCulloch,* the collier *Nansham,* and the supply ship *Zafiro* left Hong Kong for an anchorage at Mirs Bay, thirty miles away. The next day the *Olympia, Raleigh,* and *Baltimore* followed. On the *Olympia* with Commodore Dewey was a new friend who was to go through the battle with him— a chow dog he had bought in Hong Kong and named Bob.

And it was on that day, the 25th of April, 1898, that Dewey received from Secretary Long the cable that he had long been expecting:

> War has commenced between the United States and Spain. Proceed at once to Philippine Islands. Commence operations particularly against the Spanish fleet. You must capture vessels or destroy. Use utmost endeavor.

Never, as later events were to prove, was any order carried out more literally.

The ships were ready. The officers and crew were

ready. Dewey himself was eager for the test of strength and strategy that he knew lay ahead of him. But Consul Williams, who, Dewey hoped, would bring later information than any that had been contained in his communications, had not yet arrived. For two days the squadron waited. On the morning of the 27th the tug *Fame* was sighted with Williams aboard. The commanding officers of all the ships in the squadron were summoned to the flagship for a conference, at which Williams would be present, and at the same time the vessels were ordered to prepare for immediate departure.

At 2 P. M., with the captains back on their vessels, and Williams on board the *Baltimore,* the *Olympia* raised her anchor. The band struck up the stirring march from "El Capitain" and the ship was underway, with the Commodore's pennant at the main mast and the Stars and Stripes at the main peak. At the same time the *McCulloch* and the *Raleigh* got into motion, the latter taking a position on the starboard quarter of the flagship, and the former about a hundred yards behind her, with the *Baltimore* quickly moving up on the *Raleigh's* port side. Thus, in complete order, the ships fell into the places that had already been assigned them. They were in two columns, with the fighting ships leading and the supply ship and collier bringing up the rear.

The course was set for Manila Bay, six hundred miles away. George Dewey knew that he was headed either for death or for an event that would record his name in history as something more than "just another naval officer."

Chapter 12
The Battle of Manila Bay

In the mind of George Dewey, who had learned everything he could about the Philippines, there was a clear picture of the sea and land area that his squadron was approaching. He knew that Manila Bay, though the opening to it was narrow, broadened to a navigable width of twenty miles, and that there were several islands in the passage between it and the open sea. Two of these, Corregidor (which was to become famous in World War II) and Caballo divided the entrance into two channels. One, Boca Chica, was two miles wide. The other, Boca Grande, would have been twice this width had it not been for the small island within it called El Fraile, which reduced the passage to a width of about three miles. The city of Manila, he knew, lay some twenty-five miles east of the entrance. A headland called Sangley Point, and the Cavite naval station were five miles nearer.

He also knew that, before reaching the entrance to Manila Bay he must pass Subig Bay, thirty miles north of Corregidor, excellently situated for defense.

The reports he had received from Consul Williams

and others indicated that Manila, Corregidor, El Fraile, and the Cavite Naval Station were all strongly fortified, and that the entrances to both Manila Bay and Subig Bay were heavily mined. He had also been told that the Spanish squadron had sailed for Subig Bay determined to make its stand there.

Farragut must have been in his mind as his ships sailed slowly, at a speed made necessary by that of the supply steamer and the collier, toward Manila. He must have remembered how, at the Battle of Mobile Bay when some of the ships hesitated and started to veer off because of the Confederate torpedoes, Farragut had shouted, "Damn the torpedoes! Go ahead!" Substitute the word "mines" for "torpedoes" and you have an accurate idea of Commodore Dewey's attitude as he contemplated engaging the Spaniards either at Subig or Manila Bay.

As the squadron proceeded southward, rigorous training of the crew continued. They were drilled in taking their battle stations quickly, in their duties in case of fire, and in repairing possible injuries to the ships by shell fire. The positions of the gun crews were protected by barricades of canvas and iron, and the sides of the ships and the ammunition hoists were hung with festoons of heavy sheet chain. Heavy wire cables in the rigging were connected by zigzag ropes so that if one were shot in two it would not fall on the deck and possibly injure crew members. The carpenter made a number of "shot plugs" with which to stop up any holes in the hull of the ship made by enemy shells, and stretchers on which to carry the wounded to the sick bay. Life preservers and other buoyant objects, including buoyant mattresses and cushions from the life boats, were arranged so that they would float in case the ship was sunk, and give the men something to which to cling in the water. All the sails in the sail loft were banked in heavy folds on the forecastle, as a protection from rifle bullets for the men stationed in that exposed position. The life boats were wrapped in canvas to prevent flying splinters from injuring the men in case the boats were hit. At night a single light on the taffrail, carefully shielded so that it could be seen only from the rear, denoted the position of each ship. All the rest of the vessel was in darkness.

When land was sighted early on the morning of April 30, the flagship signaled the *Boston* and *Concord* to proceed at full speed as advance scouts to Subig Bay. Later some of the officers thought they heard gunfire from the direction of the Bay and, though Dewey himself had not heard it, he sent the *Baltimore* to support the two other ships if necessary. The rest of the squadron cruised slowly, waiting anxiously for the scouts to return to report.

At daylight the coast of Luzon was clearly in view, beautiful in the bright morning sunlight, and Dewey recalled later how its faint, seemingly blue hills, looking as though they faded into the sky in the distance, reminded him of the Green Mountains of Vermont, where he was born, and aroused a sense of homesickness in him. But still there was no sight of the three ships that had been sent to Subig Bay. That afternoon, however, they appeared with the report that no enemy vessels had been found.

Obviously, then, the Spanish squadron was in Manila Bay. The Commodore turned to Lamberton and said, "Now we have them!" He knew that the issue would be joined in the place that he felt would be most advantageous to the American squadron.

Later he learned that Admiral Montojo, commander of the Spanish squadron, had indeed taken his ships to Subig Bay on April 15. Considering it better suited for defense than Manila Bay he had earlier given orders for strengthening the position with additional shore batteries and mines in the harbor. But when he reached the Bay he found that his orders had not been carried out. Only a few mines had been placed in position, and four large guns, which should have been mounted a month earlier, were still lying on the beach.

Frustrated and angry, he considered what would be his best plan. At first he thought that he would hide there, hoping that the Americans would pass the Bay without entering it. In that case he planned a sudden sortie, catching them unprepared. But on the 28th he received a cable from the Spanish Consul at Hong Kong:

> The enemy's squadron sailed at 2 P. M. from the Bay of Mirs, and according to reliable accounts they sailed for Subig Bay to destroy our squadron and then will go to Manila.

That cable was enough to change his plans. The truth was that the great depth of the water at Subig would mean that when one of his ships was sunk its crew would be drowned. He also thought longingly of the shore batteries on Corregidor, Cavite, El Fraile, and at Manila, which would give him very much more protection than the inadequate defenses at Subig. He held a conference with the captains of his ships, all of whom agreed with him, and immediately turned tail and hurried back to Manila Bay. He did not anchor at Manila, which was most strongly protected by shore guns, because he knew that if he did shells from the American ships would do great damage to the capitol, but stopped at Cavite.

When the American scout ships, which had reconnoitered Subig Bay, rejoined the squadron they were only thirty miles from Corregidor. But since Dewey had decided to enter the Bay under cover of darkness, hoping thus to escape notice from the batteries that guarded it, the ships were stopped and their officers ordered by signal to come aboard the flagship.

The conference was extremely brief.

"We shall enter Manila Bay tonight," Dewey told them, "and you will follow the motions and movements of the flagship, which will lead."

According to Dewey's report in his autobiography, that was all. So thorough had been the preparations and the drilling of the officers and men in their duties that no discussion was necessary.

An account related by Laurin Hall Healy and Luis Kutner, in their biography of Dewey, *The Admiral* (Ziff-Davis, 1944), adds a story of more than ordinary human interest, said to have been told by Stephen Decatur VII, who had it from his close friend Captain William Winder.

According to this account Winder, then a lieutenant on the *Baltimore* and a nephew of Commodore Dewey, saluted his uncle and said:

"Commodore, I have always made it a policy never to take advantage of our being related. But in this instance I should like to make an exception. We think the bay is mined. I should like the privilege of commanding the *Zafiro*. She has the largest displacement of any of our ships. I could soon find out if the bay is mined, and if it is, I should have cleared a way for the squadron. Sir, this is the one chance I have to become famous."

The Commodore looked at him fondly, was silent for a moment, then said, "Billy, I have waited sixty years for this opportunity. And much as I like you and know you are a fine officer—mines or no mines, I am leading the squadron in myself. Good luck, my boy."

With a respectful salute Winder stepped back and returned to his ship with the other officers of the *Baltimore*.

The story, though it concerns a young man and his uncle, is also an indication of Commodore Dewey's relations with his subordinate officers, whose complete loyalty he had won by his fairness, his concern for the welfare of every member of his command, the thoroughness with which he foresaw and prepared for averting danger to them, his courage, and his qualities of splendid leadership. It is probable that not one of them would have hesitated to risk his own life in order to save that of his Commodore.

And the story demonstrates something else. Though

the Commodore, in refusing his nephew's request, intimated that it was because he himself wanted to earn the fame of leading the squadron, it is more likely that he was simply refusing to pass on to another officer the danger that he knew would be encountered by the first ship to enter the channel if it was mined. He had not been in combat since the Civil War, when he was a youth and simply the executive officer of one ship. Now he was thirty-six years older, only two years away from the age of retirement, and was responsible for every man in the Asiatic Squadron, which was about to enter a hazardous conflict. George Dewey faced his own dragons and assumed to the last detail every responsibility that had been entrusted to him.

Another story demonstrating the devotion of Dewey's crews to their Commodore is told by John Barrett. Barrett was United States Minister to Siam from 1894 to 1898. As a special war correspondent, representing the *New York Journal*, *Chicago Tribune*, *Boston Globe*, *Philadelphia Press*, and *San Francisco Examiner*, he accompanied the squadron to Manila Bay and was with it throughout the action. Later he wrote the book, *Admiral George Dewey*, which was published by Harper and Brothers in 1899. In it he said:

"Standing one day in the superstructure of the *Olympia*, I said to the gunner who had charge of one of the big eight-inch rifles of the forward turret:

" 'Where did you think you were going, and what did you expect to do when you sailed away from Mirs Bay?'

" 'Go and do?' he replied, with a scornful expression and tone that made me feel quite insignificant and ashamed for asking such a foolish question. 'Damn little did I or anyone else on this ship care so long as the old man was ordering it. We knew that we were going to a hot place, and meant to make it hotter for the Spaniards. But, man, we would have sailed straight into hell after him!' "

To this day no one knows whether the entrance to the bay had actually been mined or not. An officer on the *Baltimore*, Lieutenant John M. Ellicott, told in an article published in 1900 of a chart captured at Cavite which showed clearly that Boca Grande was heavily mined. He also reported that Spanish officers to whom he had talked confirmed this fact. Ellicott expressed the opinion that, though the mines were there, they had become ineffective from accumulations of barnacles and seaweed, if contact mines, or, if they were electrically controlled, the firing devices had either not been installed or had been faulty. On the other hand, Rear Admiral Bradley A. Fiske, who, at the time of the Battle of Manila Bay, had been a young lieutenant on the *Petrel*, denied that the mines had ever been placed, saying that they were found lying in the Cavite arsenal unfinished.

But whether the passage was mined or not the darkened *Olympia* steamed through it. The *Baltimore* followed, and the rest of the ships, in their prescribed positions, approached the entrance apparently unnoticed. Then, as John T. McCutcheon, who was aboard the *McCulloch*, later reported the story:

"The soot in the funnel of the *McCulloch* caught fire and this circumstance may have revealed the movements of the fleet to the enemy. The flames shot up out of the funnel like the fire of a rolling mill chimney. For a minute or two it burned, and then settled down to . . . black rolls of smoke.

"A faint light flashed up on land and then died out. A rocket leaped from Corregidor and then all was darkness and stillness again. The nervous tension at this time was very great. Again the flames rolled forth from the *McCulloch's* funnel, and then again gave way to smoke. . . . While it burned it made a perfect target for the enemy. Still there was no firing."

Suddenly, just after 12:15 o'clock, the batteries of El Fraile spoke, and a shell exploded between the *Petrel* and the *Raleigh*. The guns of the *Boston*, the *Concord*, the *Raleigh*, and the *McCulloch* answered and the El Fraile batteries lapsed into silence.

"During the fighting," McCutcheon reported, "there was the best of order on the *McCulloch*, and no one seemed to lose his head. Chief Engineer Randall was overcome by a nervous shock, probably apoplectic in character, and a few minutes after two o'clock he died."

This, incidentally, was the only action in which the *McCulloch* was engaged at Manila, for the Commodore placed her, along with the *Nanshan* and *Zafiro* (since there was no reserve ammunition for them to carry), in a secluded part of the bay where they would not be likely to sustain injury, and would not hamper the action of the rest of the squadron, and she took no part in the actual battle the next day.

The squadron, led by the flagship, headed for Manila, but when Dewey saw only merchant ships there, he changed course, swinging in a wide arc with the *Baltimore*, the *Raleigh*, the *Petrel*, the *Concord*, and the *Boston*, following in that order, headed for Cavite.

At a few minutes after five on the morning of May first, three of the Manila batteries opened fire, but their shots passed well over the American ships. The *Boston* and *Concord* each sent two shots back. The other ships, their captains bearing in mind the Commodore's warning that the squadron's supply of munitions might prove inadequate, held their fire. Dewey had reminded them again and again that they were 7,000 miles from home and that, if their ammunition became exhausted before the end of the battle, they would have no means of replenishing it. Furthermore, he told them, the objective was the destruction of the Spanish squadron, not the shore fortifications. He knew that if the Spanish fleet could be destroyed Manila would be helpless.

As daylight broke Dewey saw what he had been looking for. There they were, drawn up in a curving line off Cavite—the *Reina Cristina* (Admiral Montojo's flagship), the *Castilla*, the *Don Juan de Austria*, the *Don Antonio de Ulloa*, the *Isla de Luzón*, the *Isla de Cuba*, and the *Marqués del Duero*. Two other Spanish ships, the *Velasco* and the *Lezo*, were on the other side of Cavite Point. Some of the Spanish vessels were in motion. Others were stationary with their guns pointed at the approaching American ships.

Dewey had explained his plan fully to the captains of all his ships, and had issued an order that no shots were to be fired until the squadron was so close to the Spaniards that the assault would be most effective, and then they were to fire as rapidly as possible. The signal would be given by a shot from the *Olympia*.

All during the American squadron's slow approach to the Spaniards, the Manila batteries kept up their ineffective fire. At 5:15 the Cavite guns and those of the Spanish ships opened fire, but still the American vessels continued to steam in silence, closer and closer to their objective, their starboard batteries trained on the enemy. Two Spanish submarine mines exploded, but they were two miles ahead of the American column.

Dewey turned to Lamberton, and said with a smile, "Evidently the Spaniards are already rattled." After the battle a Spanish officer told him that the mines had been exploded only to make maneuvering of their own ships in the area safe.

At 5:40, when the American line of ships, now in close formation, with only 200 yards separating them from one another, were within a distance of 5,000 yards from the Spaniards, the Commodore turned to the captain of the *Olympia* and gave the famous command which, within a few weeks, was being repeated by thousands of hero-worshipping boys in the United States:

"You may fire when you are ready, Gridley."

Dewey himself remained in an exposed position on the bridge, with three other officers of the ship, while

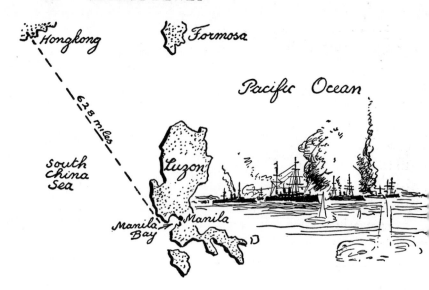

Gridley took up his station in the conning tower from which he gave the order. The first gun to speak was one of the *Olympia's* eight-inchers on the forward turret. Immediately all of the other ships began to pour shells on the Spanish ships.

Having passed them, the *Olympia* turned and started back in the direction from which she had come, with all the other ships following. Now their port guns went into action, pouring a deadly fire into the Spanish ships. The maneuver was repeated until three runs had been made from the east and two from the west. Both the *Don Juan de Austria* and the *Reina Cristina* made what Dewey himself called "brave and desperate attempts" to charge the *Olympia*, but the destructive fire from the American ships drove them back. Dewey later learned that one shell from

Battle of Manila Bay

the *Olympia* had put twenty men out of action on the *Reina Cristina* and completely demolished her steering gear. Another, which landed in her forecastle, killed several members of the crews of four rapid-fire guns and disabled the rest. A third set fire to her lowest deck (the orlop). Another shot away her mizzen mast from which the ensign and the admiral's flag flew. Still another exploded in one of the munitions rooms, and one in the sick bay, filled with wounded.

The grim story of what the American squadron had done to Admiral Montojo's flagship was revealed when she was raised from the bed of the sea five years later. In the sick bay there were eighty skeletons. There were fifteen holes made by American shells in her hull, and her upper works were a shambles. Reports after the battle showed that 150 of her men had been killed, and 90, of whom 7 were officers, wounded. Among the killed was "her valiant captain"—Dewey's words—Don Luis Cadarso. While she was on fire, and sinking, with her guns disabled, Admiral Montojo transferred himself and his flag to the *Isla de Cuba*, taking with him as many of the living among his crew as he could.

The cloud of smoke that hung over the Spanish Squadron during the battle made it almost impossible for anyone on the American ships to estimate the damage that had been done while the battle continued. At 7:45, so far as Commodore Dewey could see, the enemy ships were all still intact and in fighting shape. And it was then that a most disturbing report came to him.

Captain Gridley had sent a crew member to find out how many rounds of ammunition were left for the five-inch guns. Now he came to the Commodore and reported, with some little anxiety, that there were only fifteen round for each gun. This was what Dewey had feared most of all in contemplating the coming battle. He immediately signaled the squadron to retire "for breakfast." As the command was given by Captain Gridley, one of the *Olympia's* gunners shouted, "For God's sake, Captain, don't stop now. Let's finish 'em right off."

In spite of the protest, the *Olympia* led the squadron out of range of the Spanish guns, with the Commodore feeling the most intense moment of anxiety that he knew throughout the entire battle. But now the smoke lifted somewhat and he had a better opportunity to see the damage that his ships had wrought in a little less than two hours of battle. Some of the Spanish vessels were on fire, others were sinking, and some were retiring slowly to protection behind Cavite Point.

As the American ships passed out of range, Dewey's Chinese attendant, Ah Mah, brought him a cup of hot coffee. Beside him came Bob, the chow, wagging his tail furiously and showing his pleasure in being close to his master. It was almost as though the dog were saying, "Good shooting."

From below, the stokers, who had been working in temperatures that had reached as high as 200 degrees Fahrenheit, struggled upward for a breath of air, and flung themselves down exhausted.

In the outer bay Dewey signaled the commanders of the other ships to come aboard. For one thing he wanted to check their ammunition supply, and, hoping that other ships had more than the *Olympia,* perhaps make a redistribution of it.

One by one the captains reported the state of their vessels and of their crew. The small amount of damage that had been done by the Spaniards amazed them all: the *Baltimore* had sustained five hits and had eight men slightly wounded, none killed; the *Boston,* four minor hits, none wounded or killed; the *Concord,* no hits and no injuries. And so it went. The American squadron had been little more than scratched, so to speak. The information was signaled to the other ships, and cheer after cheer rang out across the bay.

Then came another piece of extraordinarily good news. The crew member in charge of the ammunition racks had been asked how many rounds of ammunition for the five-inch guns were still available. In the din of battle going on overhead, mingled with the noise of the engines, he had understood the question to be "How many rounds have been fired?" and had answered fifteen. Actually there were still eighty-five rounds left in the racks.

That news, along with the lack of any serious damage to the ships, brought happiness to all aboard, and before going back into action, now with complete confidence of success, everyone, including the chow, Bob, had a good breakfast while the men discussed further the slight damage that had been done to the squadron.

The hull of the *Olympia* had been struck by shells five times, and her rigging had been shattered in several places, but no serious damage had been done. One six-pounder had struck immediately under the place where Commodore Dewey had been standing, but had not harmed him.

The *Baltimore* had also been hit five times by Spanish shells, and it was one of these that had wounded two officers and six men—but none of them seriously. It had followed an almost unbelievably strange course. Entering the ship's starboard side forward, just above the line of the main deck, it had cut through the hammock netting, gone

George Dewey's chow, Bob

down through the steel deck, been deflected by a steel beam in a stateroom, turned upward to pass through the after engine room, disabled a six-inch gun, struck and exploded a box of ammunition, and finally dropped on deck.

The *Boston* had been hit four times, one shell causing a fire that had been quickly put out, and the *Petrel* had been struck once.

At 11:16 the squadron went back into action, but there was little left to do. Of the Spanish forces only the little *Ulloa* and the shore batteries were left. Both opened fire but the *Ulloa*, on which all the American guns concentrated, soon "went down gallantly with her colors flying," as Dewey later put it. The American squadron then set in close to Sangley Point, the batteries of which were so mounted that the guns could not be brought to bear at close range. Apparently when they had been installed the Spaniards had thought it impossible that any enemy ships would dare to come in so close. All of the shells fired from this point passed over the Americans and the guns were soon silenced.

The *Concord* was then sent to destroy a large transport, the *Mindanao*, which had been beached, and the *Petrel*, which had a very light draft, went into the harbor of Cavite to destroy any ships that might be found there. After a few shots, fired from her six-inch guns, the Spanish flag on the government buildings was hauled down and a white flag run up. Admiral Montojo, himself wounded, and on shore with most of the officers and men who remained under his command, had lost 381 officers and crew, as well as his ships. He knew that further resistance was useless.

At 12:30 the *Petrel* signaled the surrender and the firing ceased, while from every ship in the American squadron rose volley after volley of cheers. The crews had "followed the old man" and, as they had been sure they would, had won a complete and overwhelming victory. As for Commodore Dewey, his order to "destroy the Spanish fleet" had been carried out to the letter. The Battle of Manila Bay was over.

That night the Commodore wrote in his diary: "Reached Manila at daylight. Immediately engaged the

Spanish ships and batteries at Cavite. Destroyed eight of the former, including the *Reina Cristina* and *Castilla*. Anchored at noon off Manila." (In his official report he stated the time of anchoring off Manila as 12:40.) None of the deep satisfaction that he felt, no sense of pride in his own splendid accomplishment as the trainer and leader of his men, is reflected in the entry, nor did it later appear in his official report of the battle. Only the bare facts.

In the official report Dewey wrote that no men had been killed in the battle and only seven wounded (though in his autobiography he tells of six men and two officers wounded aboard the *Baltimore*). He did not mention the death of the *McCulloch's* chief engineer, reported by McCutcheon.

Dewey had many times proved his courage, his honesty, and his ability to handle men with a firm authority, yet with a most extraordinary sense of fairness and human kindness. Now, as one who had won an overwhelming victory in one of the decisive battles in world history, he was to show his chivalry as well. It was displayed in many acts of courtesy to the defeated Spaniards after the battle, and in this paragraph that he later wrote in his autobiography:

"Valor the Spaniards displayed, and in the most trying and adverse circumstances. The courageous defence made by all the vessels of the Spanish Squadron, the desperate attempt of the *Reina Cristina* to close with the *Olympia*, and the heroic conduct of her captain, who, after fighting his ship until she was on fire and sinking, lost his own life in his attempt to save his wounded men, can only excite the most profound admiration and pity."

Although the extent of the tragedy that befell the Spanish fleet in Manila Bay was more the fault of the shortcomings and negligence of the Spanish government than of Admiral Montojo, the Spaniards needed a scapegoat. So they recalled their admiral and submitted him to a courtmartial trial for having surrendered to the American fleet. Montojo immediately wrote Commodore Dewey stating a number of incontrovertible facts in connection with the battle and asking Dewey to confirm them, so that he might use the confirmation as evidence in his defense.

The courteous and chivalrous victor immediately complied with the request, ending his letter with this testimonial to Montojo's courage:

"I have already reported to my government that your defense of Cavite was gallant in the extreme. The fighting of your flagship, which was singled out for attack, was especially worthy of a place in the traditions of valor of your nation . . . I assure you that I very much regret that calumnies have been cast at you, and am confident that your honor cannot be dimmed by them."

Later Dewey recorded the satisfaction he felt when he learned that this letter had been instrumental in influencing the court that Montojo had fulfilled his duty in a courageous manner.

Chapter 13
Blockade and the Taking of Manila

Though the Battle of Manila was over, George Dewey's job there was not finished. A blockade still must be maintained in order to keep supplies from reaching Manila. Also the U.S. Army must come to take the city, and the squadron must be ready to co-operate with it. Dewey knew that he could take it himself, but he had not sufficient men to occupy it and maintain order. Also he wanted to save the precious ammunition that he had left in case of a possible attack from another Spanish squadron that might appear to renew the battle.

Indeed on May 20 the Navy Department cabled him a report that two Spanish warships and some transports had left Spain for the East, and on June 18 that the Spanish Camara's squadron, consisting of two armored cruisers, six converted cruisers, and four destroyers, was apparently on its way to Manila. But when Camara received news that a United States squadron of six warships was proceeding at full speed toward the Spanish coast, he turned back. Meanwhile Dewey's squadron had been reinforced by several vessels sent from the United States, and his anxiety over the possible arrival of Camara was ended.

But this is getting ahead of the story.

On the afternoon of May first, immediately following the Spanish surrender, the captain of one of the British ships in the harbor took a message from Commodore Dewey to the Spanish captain-general, Don Basilio Augustin Davila, in Manila. In it the Commodore said that if another shot were fired at the American ships from the Manila batteries, the squadron would destroy the city by gunfire. He said, too, that if the Americans were permitted to use the cable to Hong Kong, the Spaniards would also be permitted to use it.

The Captain-General immediately sent back assurances that no more shots would be fired at the American squadron, but refused to permit the use of the cable to Hong Kong. After receiving this reply Dewey ordered the *Zafiro* to cut the cable. Thus both the Spaniards and Americans were cut off from direct cable contact with the world, and it was not until May 4 that Dewey was able to send the *McCulloch* to Hong Kong with a cable containing a detailed report of the victory.

A few days after the battle Dewey received a message from Captain-General Davila intimating that he was willing to surrender the city to the Americans, but, without sufficient troops to occupy it, and unwilling to risk the sacking of the city by the rebel forces, which were pushing more and more closely toward the capital, Dewey decided not to accept the surrender but to wait for reinforcements from the United States in the form of additional ships and land troops.

Before the cable had been cut, newspaper correspondents had managed to get messages through, and Dewey learned later that on the second of May Senator Proctor of Vermont, who had recommended him for the Asiatic Squadron, wrote President McKinley this note:

"I feel well this morning.

"You may remember that you gave, at my earnest request, the direction to Secretary Long to assign Commodore Dewey to the Asiatic Squadron. You will find you made no mistake; and I want to say that he will be as wise and safe, if there are political duties devolving on him, as he is forcible in action. There is no better man in discretion and judgement. We may run him against you for President. He would make a good one."

Dozens of congratulatory cables and letters flowed in after the news became known throughout the United States. One of "the most gratifying" as Dewey put it in his autobiography was this: "Every American is your debtor. Roosevelt."

Immediately President McKinley gave Dewey the rank he should have been given when he took command of the squadron; his commodore's pennant was pulled down, to be replaced by that of an acting rear-admiral.

On the afternoon of May 2, the day after the battle, John T. McCutcheon took a dinghy and made a trip about the bay. This is what he found, as he later reported it:

"The *Castilla* shows only one upright funnel and two

burnt and charred masts. The other funnel is leaning over against the standing one, and only a few inches of shattered and crushed rail shows above the water line. The insides are burnt out completely, only the blackened iron work being visible . . .

"The *Reina Cristina* . . . lies a little farther away, as completely demolished as the *Castilla*. Her funnels are perforated, her rigging cut, and big gaping holes in the shattered steel framework show how accurate was the aim of the Americans . . . A little fire is burning on her, and the body of a Spaniard is lying halfway out of a gun barbette, his legs shot off and big slashing wounds in his hip. He is absolutely naked except for a narrow belt and has apparently been untouched by fire . . . A live chicken is perched on a stanchion at the bow. How in the world it lived through the fire is a wonder, for the vessel is absolutely gutted.

The "Reina Cristina" (from a photograph taken shortly after the battle)

"The *Antonio de Ulloa* is almost entirely under water . . . The three masts still stand, splintered by shells. Her rigging is shattered in many places. . . . Boatloads of officers and seamen have been to her all afternoon searching for souvenirs of the battle. Scraps of signal and boat flags, charts, books, small anchors, and dozens of little relics have been eagerly seized. Sailors have been diving down and bringing up all sorts of trophies, from clocks and compasses to chairs and capstan heads . . .

"A trip to the waters beyond the arsenal revealed even greater havoc and ruin. This is in Bakor Bay and is the principal anchorage of the naval station. There are seven warships, ranging from 800 tons up to 1500, scattered around in this cove, all sunken and most of them charred by flames . . . These ships were among the finest of their class in the Spanish navy."

This was the once proud Spanish squadron that even the friendly British officers at Hong Kong had thought would destroy the American ships! But George Dewey was not a man to gloat over victory. Such descriptions of devastation as this one by McCutcheon were left to the newspapermen, while Dewey busied himself with the problems of maintaining his blockade of Manila harbor, and occupying Cavite arsenal.

When he learned that, in spite of the Captain-General's assurance that no more shots would be fired by the Manila batteries, they were still manned with their guns trained on the American ships, he removed his squadron and anchored off Cavite, out of effective range for the Manila guns, in order, as he put it, "to remove the temptation."

In blockading a harbor it is internationally understood that the blockading power has the right to assign ships of other nations to anchorages outside the area of possible naval operations. After the Battle of Manila Bay men-of-war from several European powers arrived in the harbor. The proper procedure was for each ship to stop, allow an officer from the American squadron to come aboard, and assign her position.

All co-operated with Rear Admiral Dewey with the exception of the Germans. On May 6 the German man-of-war *Irene* arrived, steamed past the *Olympia*, and dropped anchor in a place of her own choice. On the same day the German transport, *Darmstadt*, brought fourteen hundred men as replacements for German crews. On the ninth a second German warship, the *Cormoran*, came in at three in the morning, and followed the same procedure. When a launch was sent out with men to board her, she paid no attention to it but steamed on, until the *Raleigh* fired a shot across her bows. To an indignant German captain the rules of blockade were then carefully explained, and she was assigned an anchorage. On the ninth, the German Vice-Admiral von Diedrich arrived aboard his flagship the *Kaiserin Augusta*. When Dewey paid a courtesy call on the Vice-Admiral he was received coolly and with no show of friendliness. It was clear, as it actually had been from the time when war between Spain and the United States began to seem inevitable, that Germany was ready to seize any opportunity that presented itself to take over the Philippine Islands herself.

At one point, according to Murat Halstead, who was on the scene during the blockade and later wrote *The Life and Achievements of Admiral Dewey*, the Admiral took it upon himself to threaten war with Germany. Halstead was on the *Olympia* at the time and overheard the threat. (It was characteristic of Dewey, as has already been shown, that he consulted no one before making his provocative statement.) The German ships had been a continual annoyance, and everyone on board the American ships knew that the German officers were making a great show of friendliness to the Spanish authorities in Manila, and in many ways violating the international rules prescribing the conduct of neutrals.

One day a German officer came aboard the *Olympia* to complain about restrictions placed on the movements of German ships by the blockading American squadron. After a long argument, in which Dewey was firm, yet tried to keep his temper, he burst out:

"Tell your Admiral I am blockading here. Now note carefully what I say. I am making this blockade as easy for everybody as I can, but I am getting tired of the puerile work here . . . Tell your Admiral that the slightest infraction of any rule will mean but one thing. That will be war . . . If your people are ready for war with the United States they can have it at any time."

After that the officers of the German Squadron, from Admiral von Diedrich down, were somewhat more careful.

The officers and crews on board all of the American

ships were kept on a constant alert, all watches rigorously kept, and the movements of any ships or smaller vessels in the Bay instantly reported, and, if there was any irregularity, it was investigated. America was still at war with Spain and George Dewey was taking no chances of having to deal with a surprise attack.

Yet for officers and men who were not, for the moment, on a specific duty, there were times of relaxation, too. Ferry boats ran regularly between Cavite and Manila, and invariably steered a course that brought them close to the *Olympia*, so that the passengers could admire her sleek lines, see the holes that Spanish shells had made in her hull, and occasionally catch a glimpse of Admiral Dewey in his white uniform on the quarterdeck. And this fact gave the officers of the squadron a splendid idea.

Each ship had a launch, but it was, in general, reserved for the use of high ranking officers. The junior officers, however, were permitted to use the lifeboats when they went on shore leave, and this they did, but soon found a way to avoid the long and arduous row from ship to shore. Three or four officers would get into one of the boats and place it in the line that was followed by the Cavite-Manila ferry. Then, when the ferry came by, they would throw a line aboard, where it was made fast at the stern, and with the officers sitting in the stern of the small boat in order to keep the bow high, they would have a jolly ride across the bay to Manila, and later back to their ship. Sometimes three or four boats from different ships, each containing two or three officers, would be strung in

From sketches made on board the "Olympia": at left: Ship's bell; at right: Dewey's favorite rattan deck chair, now in his cabin

line, at sufficient distance from one another to avoid collisions.

Watching them, Dewey must have been reminded of his boyhood days in Vermont when, in winter, the boys would hitch their sleds to horse-drawn bodsleds and be merrily pulled along the streets of Montpelier.

In addition to the chow dog, Bob, there was on board the *Olympia* a small monkey, which the crew regarded as a mascot. He was not the best-tempered little beast in the world, and had one day bitten one of the officers, so he was usually kept tied on the main deck. But often Dewey, who was fond of animals, would untie him, whereupon the monkey would leap with delight on the Admiral's shoulder and chatter with pleasure while the latter stroked him.

During the blockade there were a number of news-papermen in Manila with whom the Admiral maintained the most cordial relations. In addition to McCutcheon of the *Chicago Record*, Harden of the *New York World*, and Stickney of the *New York Herald* (the last of whom Dewey had impressed into service on board the *Olympia*), there were Egan of the *San Francisco Chronicle*, Davis of the *New York Sun*, Bass and Millet of *Harper's Weekly*, Sheridan and Boerlinger of the *San Francisco Call*, John Barrett, former minister from the United States to Siam, and in 1898 representing several American papers, and several others.

Barrett, in his book, *Admiral George Dewey*, tells at length how Dewey trusted the newspapermen and how they all admired him and never betrayed his trust.

"Gentlemen," he said to them, "you are left largely to your own good and experienced judgment, not only as correspondents but as American citizens, but you will always bear in mind that you must not send what would give actual aid and comfort to the enemy, or that which will unduly excite the people at home."

Barrett also tells of an incident that was typical of the Admiral's attitude. Certain movements of the German Squadron (not recorded in the book) apparently showed inimical intentions toward the Americans. The episode was, as Barrett put it, "fairly pregnant with sensational possibilities. It was assuredly teeming with news." Every correspondent wrote long dispatches about it and took them to Lieutenant Brumby of the *Olympia* who acted as censor (though Dewey sometimes overruled him and let the boys send cables that Brumby had forbidden). In such an important matter as this the Lieutenant referred them to the Admiral. Dewey read all of the dispatches, then said to the group of men who had become his friends:

"If you gentlemen wish, you can send these telegrams just as you have written them, but I hope you will not. If you forward your dispatches at this time, when our people are excited to the fever point, your news may be the influence which will inspire them to demand action on the part of the government that would not only seriously embarrass it at Washington, but me right here, and might lead to further complications and war. Now if you will let the matter alone and leave it to me I will settle it all right, we will save great excitement at home, and avoid all chances of war. Do as you think best."

The cables were not sent, the incident itself has not been recorded, nor has Dewey's tactful handling of it, but it is not by any means impossible that his wise judgment, the correspondents' co-operation, and the Admiral's tactful handling of the matter, may be credited with the fact that we were not forced to fight Germany and Spain at the same time.

There was, however, another element involved. Although the British officers at Hong Kong had been pessimistic about the chances of an American victory at Manila Bay, British statesmen had, from the first, believed in the American cause. Knowing Germany's ambitions they had made it quite clear that, in case of German intervention on the side of Spain, Britain and other European powers would fight with the Americans.

Dewey was fully aware of the delicacy involved in his relations with Aguinaldo, leader of the insurgent forces. It was the Admiral's policy to allow the insurgents to weaken the Spanish forces as much as possible, yet he was convinced that if the government of the Philippines was turned over to the insurgents after the war was over, the result would be chaos. Further he knew that no decision had yet been made by the United States as to the disposition of the islands once they had been won.

Aguinaldo, on the other hand, had announced his intention of setting up a provisional Filipino government, with himself at its head, which would fight, if necessary, to gain complete independence for the Philippines from all foreign rule.

Because of this conflict in points of view Dewey did not form any close relationship with Aguinaldo, and at no time gave him any assurance that the United States would be willing, after the victory, to turn the Philippines over to him and his group, or to grant them full independence. On one occasion the Admiral's tenuous relations with the rebel leader and the ever-present threat of serious conflict with the Germans became mixed.

When a report came in on July 6 that the Germans were interfering with rebel operations at Subig Bay, Dewey sent the *Raleigh* and *Concord* to investigate the matter. It was found that the insurgents were besieging a force of Spanish troops on Isla Grande, and the German

Irene was steaming into the bay obviously to help the Spaniards. As soon as the captain of the *Irene* saw the American vessels, he turned tail and ran. A few shots from the American ships brought about a quick surrender of six Spanish officers and five hundred men. The rebels instantly claimed that these should be their prisoners. Since the Americans did not have enough spare food to take care of six hundred additional men, and it was Dewey's policy to keep the friendship of the insurgents without making a formal alliance with them, or committing the U. S. to anything, the prisoners were turned over to the insurgents. But first the latter were made to promise that they would treat the Spaniards well according to the rules of civilized warfare.

Meanwhile the United States Army was on its way. Early in July Brigadier General Anderson arrived with the first expeditionary force, stopping on his way across the Pacific to occupy Guam without a battle. A few days later a second group of 3,600 men reached Manila Bay under the command of Brigadier General Francis V. Greene. They were landed at Paranaque, about halfway between Cavite and Manila, and out of range of the rifles of the 13,000 Spanish troops stationed in and about Manila. On July 25, Major General Merritt arrived and took supreme command of the Army.

Between the American forces and Manila were the intrenched insurgents, who now were simply obstacles in the way the Americans would have to take in their advance on the city. At once General Merritt assigned to

General Greene the delicate task of persuading the Filipinos to get out of the trenches in which they had fortified themselves. Greene accomplished his mission and American forces moved up and occupied the position formerly held by the Filipinos. On the 31st, Brigadier General Arthur MacArthur came with 4,000 more troops and placed himself under the command of General Greene.

General MacArthur had a son named Douglas, at that time eighteen years old, and with no premonition that he was to follow so closely in his father's footsteps. But forty-four years later the son, then himself a general, was also in the Philippines in command of 15,000 American soldiers, 40,000 members of the Filipino Army, and 100,000 Filipino reservists fighting the Japanese.

While the Army was preparing for its attack on the city, negotiations were going on between Captain-General Davila and Dewey for its surrender. Admiral Dewey was convinced that the Captain-General was sincere in these negotiations and that through them it would be possible to occupy Manila without bloodshed. But suddenly Davila was called home and replaced by General Firmin Jaudenes. The negotiations continued, but Jaudenes was more concerned with the possibility of "losing face" as the Chinese would put it, or, as the Spanish would say, "sacrificing his honor." He insisted upon making a show of resistance, and refused to surrender until the city was actually under attack.

Finally it was agreed that an attack would be made, but that as soon as it was launched Dewey would raise the international code signal "D. W. H. B.," meaning "Surrender." The Spaniards would then raise a white flag at a position in the city from which it could be seen by both the Army and the naval forces.

Before the attack, commanders of the foreign squadrons in the bay were ordered to shift their vessels so as to be out of the line of fire. And then came an interesting separation of the sheep from the goats. The German and French vessels took up positions north of the city far from the American ships, while the English and Japanese came to Cavite and anchored near Dewey's squadron. Thus friends of the United States (as not only the English but also the Japanese were at that time) were in one group, and those who were less friendly in another.

On the thirteenth of August, the day set for the attack, the American squadron got under way to take up their battle stations. As they passed the British squadron, the officers and men of the *Immortalité* thronged their deck, cheering the Americans. The guard was paraded and the ship's band played "Under the Double Eagle," which was Dewey's favorite march.

And then once more it was proved that between Englishmen and Americans "blood was thicker than water." As the American squadron drew up in battle formation, the British Captain Chichester in the *Immortalité* got under way, taking with him the *Iphegenia*. Majestically the two British ships proceeded toward Manila and took up a position between the American and German ships, with their guns silently trained on the Germans.

The battle for the city of Manila was soon over. At 9:35, four of the American ships opened fire, which they continued at long intervals for an hour, without any response from the fort. Meanwhile the land troops were advancing. As they neared the fort Dewey signaled "Cease firing" to his ships. The troops swarmed over the parapet of the fort and at 10:35 the Spanish flag came down and the Stars and Stripes were raised.

At eleven o'clock the *Olympia* raised the code signal "Surrender." Twenty minutes later Dewey was the first to see the white flag flying at the agreed-upon place on the city wall. The Battle of Manila was over and, for all practical purposes, the United States of America was in possession of the Philippine Islands, but there still were difficulties to be faced by George Dewey before he could leave.

If historians were to choose an exact moment at which the United States of America became a world power of the first magnitude it would be 11:20 A. M., August 13, 1898, when mighty Spain dropped to the rank of a fourth-rate power. If in addition they were to make a list of the men who had brought this about, George Dewey's name would without question stand high on it.

But there is a sad little word to be added to this. If the cable between Manila and Hong Kong had not been cut the attack on Manila would never have taken place and many lives would have been saved, for the war with Spain had really ended the day before, as we shall see in the next chapter. It is so often this way in the unhappy fortunes of war.

Chapter 14
Aftermath

Though the Spaniards had been thoroughly defeated in the Battle of Manila Bay, America was still deeply involved in its war with Spain. Also Dewey knew that the Filipino insurgents under Aguinaldo were simply waiting for the Americans to leave in order to take over the islands. There were many problems still to be solved. Dewey stayed to solve them.

Meanwhile the man whose name had been scarcely known to the American public before the Battle of Manila Bay had become a national hero at home. Throughout the country schoolboys were repeating his famous order to Captain Gridley. Over the doors of blacksmiths' shops and others were scrawled, "Deweyville." Puns used his name. On fences along country roads were written or painted, "Dewey Did it, Didn't he?" Lithographed portraits of the Admiral hung in saloons and other public places. Articles and verses in praise of him appeared in papers and magazines throughout the country. Most of the verses were merely doggerel, but others were of greater interest. One especially clever one was by Eugene F.

"Dewey Did it, Didn't he?"

Ware, a Kansas lawyer, who wrote under the pen-name of "Ironquill." It was first printed in the Topeka (Kansas) *Capital* soon after May 1, and is still frequently reprinted in accounts of the time:

> "*O Dewey was the morning*
> *Upon the first of May,*
> *And Dewey was the Admiral*
> *Down in Manila Bay;*
> *And Dewey were the Regent's eyes,*
> *Them orbs of royal blue.*
> *And Dewey feel discouraged?*
> *I Dew not think we Dew.*"

(The regent was Maria Cristina, who was at that time ruling Spain for her 12-year-old son Alfonso XIII.)

Postcards were issued bearing the slogan "Remember

the Maine" and a picture of the battleship. At her bow was attached an explosive cap, similar to that used in cap pistols. From it to the corner of the card ran a fuse. By lighting the fuse one could re-enact in miniature the blowing up of the famous ship.

Before the end of the year books about Dewey and the Battle of Manila Bay began to sprout like daffodils in the spring, and continued to do so in the next year.

Meanwhile the war went on in the Atlantic. Three days after armed action against Spain had been authorized by Congress, a squadron under Admiral Sampson left Key West, Florida bound for Cuba. When war was declared, Dewey's friend Theodore Roosevelt resigned as Assistant Secretary of the Navy and, with the rank of Lieutenant Colonel, assembled a regiment of volunteers, among whom were a number of western cowboys, later to become famous as the "Rough Riders." With them, and his superior, Colonel Leonard Wood, the Lieutenant Colonel arrived at Tampa, Florida, on June 3, to await embarkation for Cuba.

Roosevelt, when Police Commissioner of New York, had frequently been called "a dude." Now the dude had become a rough rider, and a popular song soon spread throughout the country—"The Yankee Dude'll Do."

On May 11, 1898, U. S. Marines landed at Guantanamo and established a base there, which is held by the United States to this day, and, as this is being written, is the subject of bitter dispute between the American government and the Cuban dictator, Fidel Castro.

On June 21 Army troops landed on Cuban soil.

On July 1 the "Rough Riders" under the command of Colonel (later General) Leonard Wood and Lieutenant Colonel Theodore Roosevelt, along with other troops, took San Juan Hill. Among the officers who fought there that day was Lieutenant John J. Pershing of the 10th Cavalry. (Later he led an expedition into Mexico, in 1916, to punish the Mexican raider Villa. In World War I, as a full general, the fourth man to hold that rank since George Washington, he was Commander in Chief of the American Expeditionary Forces.)

Of those who made the historic charge up San Juan Hill Pershing later wrote:

"White regiments, black regiments, Regulars and Rough Riders, representing the young manhood of the North and the South, fought shoulder to shoulder, unmindful of race or color, unmindful of whether commanded by an ex-Confederate or not, and mindful only of their common duty as Americans."

Any war is a horrible thing, but this, perhaps, is one of the few things that may make it bearable—that it brings fighting men closer together. When they are in the ranks in time of war there is little room in their hearts for old grievances and prejudices. They are simply human beings, comrades working together for a common cause. Of greater value to the United States than the conquest of the Philippines, Cuba, Guam, and Puerto Rico, was the fact that, to a large extent, the Spanish-American War wiped out much of the bitterness between North and South which had been created by the Civil War.

General Wheeler, in a hospital on the day of the fight, later asked a captain engaged in the charge up San Juan Hill, "Did you have any trouble making your men follow you up the hill?" The captain smiled and answered, "No sir, but I had considerable difficulty keeping up."

On July 3, an American squadron under the joint command of Admiral Sampson and Admiral Schley left the Spanish fleet in Santiago Bay six smouldering wrecks, completely wiping it out, as Dewey had destroyed the ships of Spain in Manila Bay.

In three days, July 25 to 28, Puerto Rico was taken by forces under Major General Nelson A. Miles.

On August 12, the day before the taking of the city of Manila, an armistice was signed between Spain and the United States.

On December 10, a peace treaty was signed in Paris. Through it the United States acquired Guam, Puerto Rico, and the Philippines, paying Spain $20,000,000 for the latter. The independence of Cuba was guaranteed, but America continued to maintain control of the Philippines until 1946, when the islands were granted independence. Our army had lost 290 men killed in battle, and 2,565 who died of disease, most of them in the tropical climate of Cuba.

The war with Spain was over, but for Admiral Dewey there were still several difficult months ahead.

Even before the taking of Manila, the victory in Cuba, and the signing of the armistice, another event oc-

curred in the Pacific, which was to have important conse-
quences in the history of the United States. With the Pa-
cific Squadron located at Manila, the need of a base in the
Pacific became evident, and on July 7, 1898, the Senate
adopted the Newlands Resolution, annexing the Hawaiian
Islands. Immediately a naval base was established at Pearl
Harbor, where the Japanese attacked the U. S. fleet on
December 7, 1941, forcing us into war. (On March 18,
1959, Hawaii became the fiftieth of the United States of
America.) Also in 1898 a move to rename the Philippines
"The Dewey Islands" failed, and as a compromise the
seashore drive in Manila was named "Dewey Boulevard."

News of the armistice reached Dewey on August 16,
1898. Five days later the cable was raised and spliced. But
meanwhile new trouble arose, and Dewey saw that both
his presence and that of the Army was still necessary in the
Philippines. The Army's refusal to allow the insurgents to
take part in the August 13 assault on Manila had angered
Aguinaldo. Now he considered the United States, rather
than Spain, the enemy, and was preparing a new revolt
against the Americans. Dewey, who had been in continuous touch with the Philippine situation, and who, even
before the war began, had informed himself as thoroughly
as possible on the affairs of the islands, felt that he was still
needed there. He knew that Luzon, which in effect had
been taken with the taking of Manila, was only one of
over 7,000 islands in the archipelago, and though most of
them were small, the eight million native inhabitants constituted a formidable group of insurgents. Even on Luzon,

Aguinaldo's forces were causing difficulties, for they had taken control of Manila's water supply immediately after the battle, and were using it as a bargaining point.

General Merritt had been ordered to Paris to attend the peace conference which was to begin its sitting in October, and Dewey, feeling strongly that his own place was still in Manila, cabled Secretary Long:

> I trust it may not be necessary to order me to Washington. Should regret very much to leave here while matters remain in present critical condition.

A week later the Navy Department replied:

> The President will respect your wishes and not direct you to leave your present duty. He desires you to communicate to General Merritt your views upon the general question of the Philippines, with such information as you have.

So Admiral Dewey stayed to finish the job he had begun. He was, as his father had told him he must, going to "do the rest himself" and do it well.

The events of the following months proved his wisdom. Aguinaldo had established headquarters, for what he called his "government," at Malolos, about twenty-eight miles from Manila. After the peace treaty was signed in Paris, giving control of the Philippines to the United States, the rebel leader, having already assumed the role of a dictator, flamed with anger against what he considered the treachery of the Americans. He had no faith whatever in President McKinley's order to Secretary of War Alger that the military governor of the islands should act as a friend rather than as a conqueror.

On January 6, 1899, Aguinaldo broke off friendly relations with the United States Army in the Philippines, and on February 4 his insurgents attacked American sentries outside Manila. In the bloody battle that followed fifty Americans and some thousand Filipino lives were lost. The operations on land were under the command of General Otis, who had succeeded General Merritt, General Ovenshine, and General Arthur MacArthur. They were supported by the guns of Admiral Dewey's squadron in Manila Bay.

A few days after the attack outside Manila the insurgents on the island of Cebu took up arms. Dewey immediately ordered the *Petrel* there and when her guns were trained on the islands, the insurgents surrendered at once. The Admiral cabled the Secretary of the Navy:

> Affairs are very disturbed in Philippine Islands. The natives are excited and frightened and being misled by false reports spread by Spaniards who should be returned to Spain as soon as possible. Strongly urge that the President send here as soon as possible Civilian Commission to adjust differences.

Again his wisdom was proved. On February 15 Aguinaldo issued a warning that insurgent troops would kill all foreigners found on the islands. "Philippine families only will be respected," he said. "They should not be molested, but all other individuals of whatever race they may be will be exterminated without any compassion. . . . War without quarter to the false Americans who have deceived us. Either independence or death." In February the insurgents attempted to destroy Manila by fire, and shot down American troops as they extinguished the blaze. Although this was not Aguinaldo's intent, only that part of the city that housed Filipinos was seriously damaged.

For two years small bands of insurgents operated ineffectively against United States forces in the Philippine hills. Finally, in March, 1901, Colonel Frederick T. Funston executed one of the most daring and fantastic hoaxes in the history of warfare. Obtaining the co-operation of a group of natives who had formerly been among Aguinaldo's troops, but who had taken the oath of allegiance to the United States, he induced them to pose as insurgents. Funston himself, and a few other Americans, posed as prisoners of the carefully instructed natives. These delivered their American "prisoners" to Aguinaldo himself on March 23. The rebel leader was quickly overpowered and captured, and, save for a few sporadic outbursts, the rebellion was ended.

But long before that date George Dewey had received an honor which has been accorded no other man in the armed forces of the United States. On March 2, 1899, following a resolution passed by the House of Representatives and also by the Senate, President McKinley was "authorized to appoint, by selection and promotion, an Admiral of the Navy, who shall not be placed upon the retired list except upon his own application; and whenever such office shall be vacated by death or otherwise, the office shall cease to exist." The measure provided that the Admiral, even if he chose to retire, should receive his full pay of $13,500 a year, plus allowances, for the rest of his life. The resolution, while it did not name Dewey, was specifically intended to apply to him, and the President immediately concurred.

George Dewey received by cable, on March 4, 1899, news of the honor which had been conferred on him. On the same day Jacob G. Schurman, Charles Denby, and Dean C. Worcester arrived, who, with Admiral Dewey formed the Philippine Commission which Dewey had recommended to the President. The Commission began at once to study the situation, held its first official session on March 20, and on April 4 issued a proclamation to the Filipinos which stated the attitude of America in its relations with the people of the islands.

The proclamation made it quite clear that the supremacy of the United States must be recognized and that it would be enforced. But it promised "the amplest liberty of self-government" that was consistent with keeping order and maintaining a stable and economical administration. It guaranteed civil liberties for the Filipinos, an honest system of civil service in which Filipinos would be employed, fair taxes, honest, fair, and prompt administration of justice, the construction of good roads, rail lines, schools, and other public works—in short the advancement in every way possible of the native welfare.

During these trying weeks Admiral Dewey found pleasant relaxation in visiting with his cousin Albert

Dewey, and his wife, who, traveling in the Orient, paid a call on Cousin George on board the *Olympia*. The two men had not seen each other for several years, and the Admiral eagerly caught up with news from home. He was amused to learn that his nephew, Charles (the son of Albert), now a freshman at St. Paul's school in Concord, New Hampshire, had won a nickname from the Battle of Manila Bay. The other boys now called him "Admiral," and he was proud of it. The story had an especial interest for Cousin George, since his own son, George Goodwin Dewey, had also been a St. Paul's boy.

Just a little more than a year from the time when Dewey and his squadron had reached Manila Bay, the Admiral of the Navy prepared to leave it. Though sporadic fighting still continued in outlying regions Dewey felt that his job had been done.

On the afternoon of May 20, 1899, the *Olympia* made ready to put to sea. Captain A. S. Barker of the *Oregon*, who was taking over Dewey's command, stood on the bridge of his ship watching the preparations. Every ship in the squadron flew bright signal flags spelling out "Bon voyage," "Good-by," and "happy sailing." On every ship the crew lined the rail facing the *Olympia*. As the ship's bell on the *Olympia* sounded eight bells (four o'clock) the Admiral turned to Captain Lamberton and said, "Weigh anchor."

As the great hook broke water, cheer after cheer sounded from the crews of the other ships, and one after

The "Olympia" leaves Manila Bay

another the guns of all the vessels roared their nineteen-gun salutes to their Admiral. As the *Olympia* passed the *Oregon* the band of the latter was playing "Home Sweet Home." The British cruiser *Powerful* rendered its nineteen-gun salute and then its band played "Auld Lang Syne" and the *Olympia's* band responded with "God Save the Queen."

There was a lump in the throat of the Admiral and his eyes were moist as the *Olympia* passed through Boca Grande channel and he looked for the last time at the hills of Luzon which were so like those of his native Vermont.

A stop was made in the harbor of Trieste, during which Dewey revived briefly an acquaintance he had made forty years before. The American Consul brought on board the autograph album of one Princess Mary de Ligouri, asking that the Admiral sign it for her. Looking through the book Dewey found the signatures of several of the officers of the *Wabash* on which he had made his midshipman's cruise in 1858. He remembered the visit of the *Wabash* to the Bosporus, and how the American Consul Williams had come on board with his daughter Mary and her autograph book. Could the Princess Mary be the former Mary Williams?

He signed the book and sent back word that if, indeed, she was the former Mary Williams, his barge was at her service. That very afternoon she came to call, confirming at once his belief, and they chatted at length of the days that were gone. Both were white-haired now, and the former Mary Williams had spent most of her adult life away from the land of her birth. But, as Dewey recorded in his autobiography, "though she had lived so long abroad she was still a good American at heart, and she declared that she had fairly crowed when she heard of our victory at Manila, because she was surrounded by Austrians who had strong Spanish sympathies, and thought that Spain would win."

At Trieste Dewey made the customary round of courtesy calls. He was entertained in the Hotel de la Ville by the United States minister at a dinner attended by all diplomats of the highest rank. And it was at the Hotel de la Ville that he was interviewed by a correspondent of the *New York Herald* who asked him whether the fact that Admiral von Dietrich had been recalled as commander of the German Pacific fleet could be interpreted as an expression of friendship to the United States.

The next day (July 28, 1899), the *New York Herald* printed the interview.

"He was relieved of his post in accordance with an arrangement of long standing, and because his time was up, not as a concession made in friendliness to the American Government. The German policy is to prevent other powers from obtaining what she cannot accept herself. We need a large and thoroughly equipped Navy that can cope with any other power. That is the only way to block such activities. Our next war will be with Germany."

Government officials were almost speechless with astonishment when they read the interview and busily proclaimed that they didn't believe that Dewey had said anything of the kind. When, however, Dewey was later asked by another correspondent whether the report was true, he answered simply "I long ago gave up denying or affirming newspaper reports." After his return home, according to *The Admiral*, by Laurin Hall Healy and Luis Kutner, he admitted to friends that the *Herald* correspondent had reported his words accurately. "I firmly believe it," he said, "and God willing I'll fight in it."

How prophetic the words were!

There was one tragedy aboard the *Olympia* during the voyage home. Some might say that it was only a little one, and not worth mentioning, but anyone who has loved and lost a dog knows better. Bob, the chow Dewey had acquired at Hong Kong, died and was given burial at sea. Later, in Washington, the Admiral got another dog and named him Bob, after the friend he had lost.

Chapter 15

A Hero's Homecoming

Long before Dewey had left Manila Bay, preparations were being made in the United States to honor him on his return. Of some of these he had heard. One of the things that troubled him was the knowledge that a group of his admirers wanted him to be a candidate for the presidency of the United States. When his cousin Albert Dewey and his wife had visited him in Manila Bay, the Admiral had turned to him for advice. "Albert," he said,

"I am in a quandary and would like your advice. There is an individual here in Manila who represents Mr. Hearst of the Hearst publications. For the past week he has been seeking an interview with me and I am informed that he has been authorized to ask me to become a candidate for the Presidency to be supported by the Hearst newspapers."

For a moment Albert Dewey was silent, then he answered gravely:

"I fear you are placing too great a responsibility on me in asking for advice on such an important question. Several facts should be carefully considered before you reach a decision. Not having been in the United States since your great victory I believe you cannot realize on what a pinnacle of esteem and affection you have been placed by the American people. Should you descend of your own accord from this pinnacle to take a place on another which the American people might think you considered higher and more important than that on which they placed you, you might lose their affection and esteem. And never forget, the public is very fickle."

George Dewey nodded in thoughtful silence. Later he issued a statement:

"I would not accept a nomination for the Presidency of the United States. I have no desire for any political office. I am unfitted for it, having neither the education nor the training . . .

"The Navy is one profession, politics another. I am too old to learn a new profession now . . . This is final."

He had also learned that Congress had voted to present him with a golden, jeweled sword, which had been tooled by Tiffany and Company, and of other plans to honor him, and felt a combination of pride and dread in looking forward to what was awaiting him when he arrived in America.

"I knew what to do in command of the Asiatic Squadron," he wrote in his autobiography, "but being of flesh and blood and not a superman, it seemed impossible to live up to all that was expected of me as a returning hero."

At Gibraltar on September 10, 1899, he had written to his son:

My dear Son:

We leave here tomorrow for New York . . . I expect to anchor off Tomkinsville [six miles from the City of New York] on the 28th and shall look for you soon after. Bring your bag and be prepared to stay aboard for a day or so . . .

I expect to go to Washington to receive the sword on Tuesday 30 October, after that to Montpelier for a reception. After that to get out of everything I can . . .

With love,

Your affectionate Father.

But his anticipation of the welcome he was to receive was dwarfed by the reality. He had read newspapers. He had received, while still abroad, invitations from cities, civic organizations, and large corporations, to attend receptions in his honor. He knew that he would have to conserve his strength by saying "no" to some of the invitations. But what he found when he reached America was far beyond what he had imagined. "On the 30th of April, 1898," he wrote, "I had been practically unknown to the general public. In a day my name was on everyone's lips."

While still at sea the *Olympia* was met by the Atlantic Squadron of the United States Navy and escorted to Sandy Hook, where on September 26 the whole squadron cast anchor. On the Brooklyn Bridge a huge electric sign bore the words "WELCOME DEWEY." Among the ships were the *Iowa, New York, Texas,* and *Brooklyn* which had defeated Cervera's fleet at Santiago. Small boats, carrying distinguished persons, arrived to greet the Admiral aboard the *Olympia*. Among them was Rear Admiral Sampson, hero of the Battle of Santiago Bay, an old friend of Dewey's, like the Admiral a graduate of Annapolis, and one who had been Dewey's shipmate on the *Colorado* after the Civil War.

The following day the squadron anchored at Tomkinsville where the Admiral's son, George, was waiting to greet him. Other visitors also came aboard—the Admiral's old friend Theodore Roosevelt, now Governor of New York, the Governors of Vermont and New Jersey, Boss Richard Croker of Tammany Hall, Chauncey Depew, president and chairman of the board of the New York Central Railroad, and a delegation headed by J. Pierpont Morgan and William Randolph Hearst, who had come aboard for the purpose of urging the Admiral to be a candidate for the Presidency of the United States.

To their proposal Dewey, at this time, said firmly, "No sir! I am a navy man and I don't want any part of it." (Later he was unfortunately to have second thoughts about the matter.)

Three days later there was a naval parade up the Hudson composed of the Atlantic Squadron headed by the *Olympia*. As the ships proceeded up river the docks, the shore, and the roofs of buildings were crowded with cheering throngs. Sirens, whistles, and foghorns of other ships and tugs in the river blared their enthusiastic praise. Turning back at 125th Street, the *Olympia* docked at 106th Street where her guns saluted the city.

Later the Admiral and his son went ashore to the Waldorf Astoria where a large suite had been engaged for him as the guest of New York.

The next day a parade of more than 35,000 men, some in uniform, some in civilian clothing, formed at 156th Street and marched down Fifth Avenue in a "Dewey parade." At its head Admiral Dewey rode in a carriage. Immediately behind him came Governor Theodore Roosevelt on horseback. A dozen bands played such songs as "Tenting Tonight," "The Battle Hymn of the Republic," and other Dewey favorites. At Twenty-third Street they came to the "Dewey Arch," an elaborate and imposing temporary structure somewhat like that of the arch in the Roman Forum commemorating the taking of Jerusalem by Titus in 70 A. D. The Chicago *Inter-Ocean* said of it, "All who have seen the monumental arches of the Old World agree that in originality, grace, animation, spontaneity, and symmetry, the Dewey Arch is worthy of perpetuity."

Here the aging Admiral dismounted and stood for over five hours receiving and returning the salutes of those passing in review. Then there were speeches and the presentation of a gigantic key to the city, and after that he was given a golden loving cup, eighteen inches high, embossed with pictures representing the victory at Manila Bay. It had been made by Tiffany from ten thousand dollars' worth of twenty-dollar gold pieces.

But this was only the beginning. From all over the country invitations were pouring in on the Admiral. A gold plaque came from Columbus, Ohio. On it was engraved:

"Christopher Columbus, on October 12, 1492, made possible the achievement of George Dewey on May 1, 1898. The capital city of Ohio, which perpetuated the great discoverer, requests the presence of the Great Admiral as its guest."

Another plaque, presented by the Grand Army of the Republic, was engraved with praise of Dewey and gave him credit for healing the wounds created by the Civil War between the North and the South. It also invited him to attend the annual reunion of the G.A.R. at Jacksonville, Illinois.

No other name in the history of America was on as many lips, or printed or engraved in as many places, as was that of George Dewey in 1899. Gold eyeglass cases, paper cutters, cigar boxes, commemorative China plates, miniature busts of the Admiral, hats, and epaulets, all inscribed with his praises, were everywhere. There were beer mugs bearing his picture, Dewey dolls, Dewey paper weights, Dewey canes. The town of Three Oaks, Michigan, set up a "Dewey Cannon" and invited the Admiral to its unveiling. Badges and commemorative medals were issued by the hundreds. There were Dewey spoons and hats. The Piccadilly Club of Cincinnati, Ohio, the city of Savannah, Georgia, and the city of St. Louis, Missouri, all sent loving cups to the Admiral.

On the Monday following the New York parade, the two George Deweys, father and son, boarded a special train for Washington. With them went a committee from the nation's capital which had been sent to New York to bring him back. All along the route stations were crowded with throngs who had gathered for the privilege of seeing the train that carried their hero.

At Washington he was greeted by a cheering crowd of over 5,000 persons. A carriage had been reserved for him and was waiting. Close by it was another in which sat Mrs. Washington McLean, and her two daughters, one of them the Admiral's old friend, the widowed Mildred McLean Hazen. They greeted him and told him that their home, "Draper House," was at his disposal during his stay for the ceremonies that had been planned for him. The Admiral demurred at putting them to any inconvenience. But when they explained that their plans had been well made, and that they had already moved out in order to give him complete freedom, he accepted their hospitality with thanks.

At the White House President McKinley and his cabinet greeted the Admiral warmly and honored him at a dinner. Later the weary hero stood on a reviewing stand as a torchlight parade passed before him. It was late that night before the tired Admiral and his son found rest in the McLean home at 1707 K Street.

The next day the impressive sword presentation took place. Thousands of admirers stood before the stand, draped with flags and buntings, which had been erected on Capitol Hill where President McKinley, his cabinet, congressmen, and senators were gathered before the Admiral arrived. As the guest of honor approached the steps leading up to the stand the President walked down them to greet him and show him to his seat. Following McKinley was Secretary of the Navy Long, carrying an oblong case.

Secretary Long gave the presentation address.

"You went, you saw, you conquered," he said, ". . . and your country strode instantly forward, a mightier power among the nations of the world."

He read the Act of Congress which had been passed immediately after the Battle of Manila Bay, before Dewey was promoted, and which authorized the Secretary of the Navy

"to present a sword of honor to Commodore George Dewey and to cause bronze medals, commemorating the Battle of Manila Bay to be struck, and to distribute such medals to the officers and men of the ships . . . under command of Commodore George Dewey on May 1, 1898, and that to enable the Secretary to carry out this resolution the sum of $10,000, or so much thereof as may be necessary is hereby appropriated. . . .

"No captain ever faced a more crucial test than when, that morning, with every foreign port in the world shut to you, with nothing between you and annihilation but the thin sheathing of your ships, your cannon, and your devoted officers and men, you moved upon the enemy's batteries on shore and on sea with unflinching faith and nerve, and before the sun was halfway up the heavens had silenced the guns of the foe, sunk the hostile fleet, demonstrated the supremacy of American sea power and transferred to the United States an imperial cluster of the islands of the Pacific

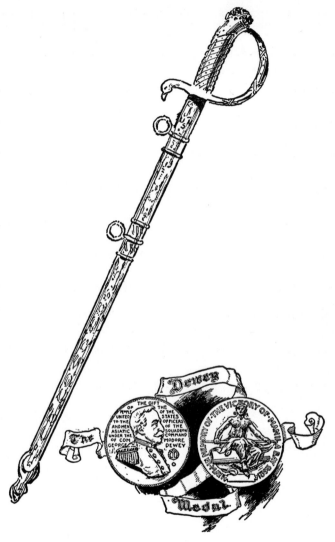

The sword presented to Admiral of the Navy George Dewey, and the Dewey medal

. . . Generations hence your name shall be . . . a household word . . . enshrined in history."

When he had finished his long speech he handed the gold, jewel-encrusted sword to President McKinley, who handed it to George Dewey. Then, taking it back, the President carefully attached it to the left side of the Admiral's sword belt.

During the few days that Dewey spent in Washington on this trip he made several calls on Mrs. Washington McLean and her two daughters.

Then he took a special train to Montpelier, Vermont where welcoming ceremonies had been prepared for him. He reviewed a parade of the State Militia, received an honorary degree of Doctor of Laws from the University of Vermont, and, by order of the State Senate, a classical laurel wreath was placed on his head. Similar honors were paid him in Boston. There he was presented with a second sword, Admiral Farragut's pennant, a watch, and the freedom of the city, and a city square was named after him.

Invitations continued to pour in from other cities all over the country, many of which the poor man had to decline because of sheer exhaustion.

America's hero had come home to such an ovation as no other had received before him.

Chapter 16

The Admiral Carries On

In 1899 George Dewey was 62 years old, and, under the rules of the Navy, would ordinarily have been retired. But the special Act of Congress by which he had been appointed "Admiral of the Navy" provided that he was to be retired only at his own request, and whether retired or active, his salary was to continue for the rest of his life. The idea of permanent inactivity was repulsive to the man whose life had been a continuous round of activity, and he was delighted when a new duty was placed upon him.

Before the Spanish-American War no central advisory body to the Navy had existed. On March 4, 1900, Secretary Long established the General Board of the United States Navy to fulfill this function. Admiral Dewey was named as its president, an office which he held until his death.

Meanwhile another important event in his life had occurred. On November 9, 1899, he had married Mildred McLean Hazen, twenty years his junior. "To her companionship," he wrote in his autobiography, "I owe my happiness in later years." After a short honeymoon, they moved into a house at 1747 Rhode Island Avenue, N.W. which had been bought with $50,000 collected by popular subscription throughout the nation and given to him as one more mark of esteem.

And still he was being urged to run for the Presidency. During the spring of 1900 newspapermen constantly sought interviews with him on the subject. *The New York World* had been a particularly faithful supporter of the plan, and on April 3, 1900 one of the *World's* Washington correspondents, Horace J. Mock, went to Dewey's home to ask once more whether he would not reconsider and seek the highest office in the land.

To Mock's surprise the Admiral answered, "Yes, I have decided to become a candidate."

But it was too late. There were two obstacles which Dewey had failed to realize. The national reception that was given to the announcement was to prove the truth of his Cousin Albert's statement about the fickleness of the public.

One of the obstacles was related to his marriage. This was at a time when "The American Protective Association," a violently anti-Catholic organization, was very active spreading vicious and unjustified charges against all Catholics, and antagonism to the Church of Rome ran high in America. When it was learned that the second Mrs. Dewey was a convert to Catholicism, anti-Catholic feeling was turned against her husband, as well as herself.

The feeling was increased through an event in connection with the house that had been given to Dewey. The Admiral decided that he would like to deed the house to his son, George Goodwin Dewey, but when he consulted his lawyer about it he learned that the terms of gift made it impossible for him to do so under the laws of the District of Columbia. He could, however, if he chose, deed it to his wife, who could in turn, deed it to his son. So Dewey signed a deed, making the house the property of his wife.

When the transfer was announced, Dewey became the object of abuse. It was said that Mrs. Dewey would manage the Admiral's campaign for the Presidency, and that the house would be made headquarters for high authorities in the Catholic Church. If Dewey were elected President, it was said, he would be ruled by the Pope in Rome.

Another element in the change of feeling toward him was his lack of political knowledge. Knowing, as he himself had said, nothing about politics, and little about government, he made statements that no trained politician would have dared to make while seeking a high office. On April 4, 1900, *The New York World* quoted him as having said:

"Since studying the subject I am convinced that the office of the President is not such a very difficult one to fill, his duties being mainly to execute the laws of Congress. Should I be chosen for this exalted position I would execute the laws of Congress as faithfully as I have always executed the orders of my superiors."

Of course the statement was foolish, showing little or no understanding of the tremendous responsibilities that rest on the shoulders of the Chief Executive of the United States. Cordell Hull, then a representative from Tennessee, and later to become Secretary of State under President Franklin D. Roosevelt, said, "I don't believe Dewey is responsible for that fool interview. If he is, he does not realize the dignity of the position of President when he says all he has to do as President is carry out the orders of Congress." Mark Hanna, who favored the re-nomination of William McKinley, said of Dewey, "Who will nominate him? Of course he has a perfect right to aspire to be nominated, but he will not be the nominee of the Republican Party."

Other honest, but politically unwise, remarks further antagonized the leaders of both major political parties, and the "Dewey for President" boom fizzled out, probably to the great relief of the Admiral, who now could devote his full time and attention to the affairs of the Navy which he loved, and which he was supremely fitted to serve. In his autobiography, published in 1912, he made no mention whatever of his Presidential aspirations, or even of the fact that he had been asked to run.

In spite of the unfavorable political comment, the general adulation of Dewey by the public continued. One aspect of it became rather a nuisance. There was scarcely a day when someone who had contributed—even though no more than twenty-five cents—to the purchase of the house given to Dewey did not ring the doorbell asking to be shown through it. Often, if Mrs. Dewey courteously asked them to come at another time, since the Admiral was resting, or because for some other reason it was inconvenient, the visitor would protest that he or she had helped to buy it and had a right to come and go at any time.

Finally the nuisance became too much for George and Mildred Dewey and they moved to the house at 1601 K Street that Mildred's father had given her.

As President of the General Board of the United States Navy the Admiral worked constantly to build a stronger fleet. Less than a month after he took office, the Navy acquired its first submarine, *The Holland* (named after its inventor), and a new era in naval warfare opened.

When McKinley was assassinated in 1901 and Theodore Roosevelt became President the Admiral gained new prestige through his friendship with the President, and their co-operation with each other, for Roosevelt called upon him often to discuss naval matters and receive his advice.

When, in 1903, the Wrights made the first brief flight in a heavier-than-air machine at Kitty Hawk, N.C., Admiral Dewey immediately saw the possibilities of the machine and pressed for government support of this new machine as a potentially powerful weapon.

Twice during his later years he went to sea again as flag officer: once in 1902, when trouble between European powers and Venezuela induced the United States to send a fleet on a cruise of the Caribbean; and again in 1903 to inspect the North Atlantic Squadron. On both of these cruises his flagship was the *Mayflower*, which later, from 1906 to 1929, was the Presidential Yacht, and, in World War II became a convoy escort vessel.

Dewey always hated public speaking, but occasionally could not avoid it. An episode connected with one of his speeches he always remembered with pleasure. Addressing the midshipmen at Annapolis, he asked, "Is there anyone here who can tell me what three ships won the Battle of Manila?" A young midshipman stood at attention and said, "I can, sir—leadership, fellowship, and seamanship." Dewey smiled and nodded with pleasure.

In 1907, the Japanese, angered by demonstrations against their people in California, protested violently to the American government. A retired Army officer, living in Russia, reported threats made by a high-ranking Japanese there that Japan was ready at any time to take the Philippines and would proceed from there to take the Pacific coast of America from California to Alaska.

After talking the matter over with the Admiral, President Roosevelt sent a fleet of sixteen American battleships on a cruise, with a stop at Tokyo. The Japanese threats ceased. The war with Japan had been put off for thirty-four years.

But Admiral Dewey was still not satisfied. He urged a more practical distribution of the United States Fleet, enabling it to be ready for instant action in case war with Japan became a reality. He pointed out that the Philippines could not possibly be held against a Japanese attack unless we could respond to it at sea instantly. He recommended that a naval base be established in Subig Bay and another at Guantanamo, Cuba. Though his recommendations were not fully carried out, the wisdom of them was proved on December 7, 1941, when Japan attacked Pearl Harbor.

When the American fleet sailed for its cruise in 1907 Dewey was not quite 70. His ill-starred, half-hearted campaign for the Presidency, and the criticism of his second marriage had been forgotten. He was still basically America's Number One hero, still busily serving his country in the profession which so well suited him. Indeed, to America as a whole he had become the beloved "Mr. Navy."

In 1912 George Dewey was seventy-five years old. He still carried on his duties as President of the General Board, still worked for a larger and better Navy, still was valued at the White House for his advice in naval matters which had preoccupied his attention and received his most careful study during all of his adult life.

In 1898 he had begun to write a book of his memoirs. Now friends urged him to continue it and he did so, with the assistance of his aide, Commander Nathan Sargent. When it was finished the *Autobiography* was published by Charles Scribner's Sons in 1913. In the Preface he wrote:

"It is fifty-nine years since I became an acting midshipman. My memory stretches from an apprenticeship under the veterans of the War of 1812, those heroes of the old sailing frigates and ships of the line; from the earliest days of the steam frigates through the Civil War; from the period of inertia in the seventies, when our obsolete ships were the byword of the navies of the world, to the building of the ships of the new navy which I was to give its first baptism of fire; and finally, to my service as head of the general board of the navy since the Spanish War.

"I have been through many administrations and have known many famous men both at home and abroad. When I entered the Naval Academy in 1854, Commodore Perry was just opening Japan to civilization; it was only six years since California had become United States territory; . . . there was yet no transcontinental railroad. At seventy-five I am writing in the hope of giving some pleasure to my country-men, from whom I have received such exceptional honors, and in the hope that my narrative may be of some value and inspiration to the young men of the navy of today, who are serving with the same purpose that animated the men of Decatur's, Macdonough's, and Farragut's day, and later, the men of our squadrons which fought at Manila and Santiago."

He had, indeed, lived through "many administrations." Born while Martin Van Buren was President, he had lived through the terms of Harrison, Tyler, Polk, Taylor, Fillmore, Pierce, Buchanan, Lincoln, Johnson, Grant, Hayes, Garfield, Arthur, Cleveland, Harrison, McKinley, and was to survive the years during which Theodore Roosevelt and William Howard Taft served, and the first term of Woodrow Wilson. Dewey had been an important factor in the history of the United States of America during one of its most significant periods of development.

Copies of the *Autobiography* reached Germany while the German government was perfecting its plans for the launching of what has since come to be known as World War I—a war that Dewey had predicted in 1899. His account of the trouble he had encountered with Admiral von Dietrich in Manila Bay immediately raised a storm of angry protest and denial. A letter from Count Reventlow was published, branding every charge that Dewey made a falsehood. Admiral von Tirpiz (who later advocated unrestricted submarine warfare during World War I) addressed the German Reichstag, accusing Dewey of malicious misrepresentation in an attempt to arouse feeling in America against "peace-loving Germany." Von Dietrich himself wrote a denial for a German publication saying that Dewey had threatened him with war, and that only his own (that is von Dietrich's) forbearance had kept the two nations from actual battle.

But Dewey, as he always had done, "stuck to his guns" and refused to modify his statements. Both Bradley Fiske, in his memoirs, *Wartime in Manila*, and Sir Edward Chichester, who had the story from his father, Dewey's friend at Manila Bay, said that Dewey's account was correct in every particular.

In 1914 Dewey was asked once more to assume command of the *Olympia* which was to be the first American ship to go through the newly completed Panama Canal, but he declined. Europe was now aflame with the war that Dewey had foreseen fifteen years before, and into which he felt that America would inevitably be drawn.

He felt that he must stay in Washington doing what he could to help prepare his country for the conflict to come. Though he participated in a New York pageant called the "Battle Cry for Peace" he continued to work at the task of building up the Navy.

In 1916 Mildred Dewey was one of the founders of the Woman's Naval Service, which was a forerunner of the WAVES, WACS, and SPARS of World War II. Admiral Dewey became advisor to the service and addressed its early members in "Dewey Hall" (so christened by the Admiral's wife) at their training camp, opened on May 1, 1916, the eighteenth anniversary of the Battle of Manila Bay.

At the beginning of 1917 George Dewey was seventy-nine years old. Woodrow Wilson, having won his election for a second term on the slogan "He kept us out of war," was in the White House. But it had become increasingly clear that nothing that Woodrow Wilson or anyone else did could continue to keep us from joining the conflict. George Dewey, wearied by his years and the load of responsibility that he had carried ever since he had left the naval academy, worked on with all the energy he could command, helping to prepare the Navy for the gigantic task he was sure lay ahead of it.

On January 11th he got up as usual, dressed, ate his breakfast and rose from the table to go to his office. As he did so he felt a sharp pain in his side. He had known them before, and often they had been more severe than this, sometimes keeping him in bed for two or three days. He said nothing about this one, told his wife good-by, and walked out the front door. Suddenly the pain came back, this time so strongly that it made him stop and put his hand to his side. His coachman, waiting at the curb, rushed from the carriage and caught the Admiral as he fell. He was put to bed, and for five days seemed at times a little better. But little by little his strength ebbed and on January 16 he died, less than three months before the United States entered the war for which he had so ably helped to prepare it.

On the high seas and in every port of the world where there were American ships the United States flag flew at half mast, as they did on land throughout the United States, and in the Philippines, where many buildings were draped in black. A resolution was introduced in the House of Representatives to change the name of the Danish West Indies to the "Dewey Islands," but it never came to a vote.

George Dewey had fought through two wars and had helped prepare his country for a third. The causes of both the Civil War and the Spanish-American War were many and complex, but perhaps, in thinking of the Admiral, the most important thing to remember is that in both he fought for freedom—in the Civil War for that of the slaves, in the war with Spain for that of the Filipinos.

Tributes to him appeared in the press throughout America and the friendly countries of Europe. But per-

His coachman caught the Admiral as he fell

haps the one which summed up his character and the nature of his service best was that uttered by President Wilson before Congress:

"It was as a commodore that he rendered the service in the action of Manila Bay which has given him a place forever memorable in the naval annals of the country. At the time of his death he held the exceptional rank of Admiral of the Navy by special act of Congress. During the later years of his life he was honored president of the General Board of the Navy, to whose duties he gave the most assiduous attention, and in which office he rendered a service to the Navy quite invaluable in its sincerity and quality of practical sagacity.

"It is pleasant to recall what qualities gave him his well deserved fame: his practical directness; his courage without self-consciousness; his efficient capacity in matters of administration; the readiness to fight without asking any questions or hesitancy about details. It was by such qualities that he continued to add lustre to the best traditions of our Navy. He had the stuff in him which all true men admire, and upon which all statesmen must depend in hour of peril.

"The whole nation will mourn the loss of its most distinguished naval officer, a man who has been as faithful, as intelligent and as successful in the performance of his responsible duties in time of peace as he was gallant and successful in time of war. It is just such men that give the service distinction, and the nation a just pride in those who serve it.

"The people and the government of the United States will always rejoice to perpetuate his name in all honor and affection."

Yes, George Dewey had done "the rest" well.

Epilogue

On Sunday, February 10, 1963, George Goodwin Dewey, the Admiral's only son, died, at the age of ninety, in Chicago, where he had lived since 1900. He was a retired cotton broker who insisted that he did not enjoy living in his father's reflected glory.

Before his death, Mr. Dewey gave the jeweled sword, presented to his father by President McKinley; a silver loving cup, made from dimes contributed by American school children; and other treasured souvenirs, to the Chicago Historical Society.

Index

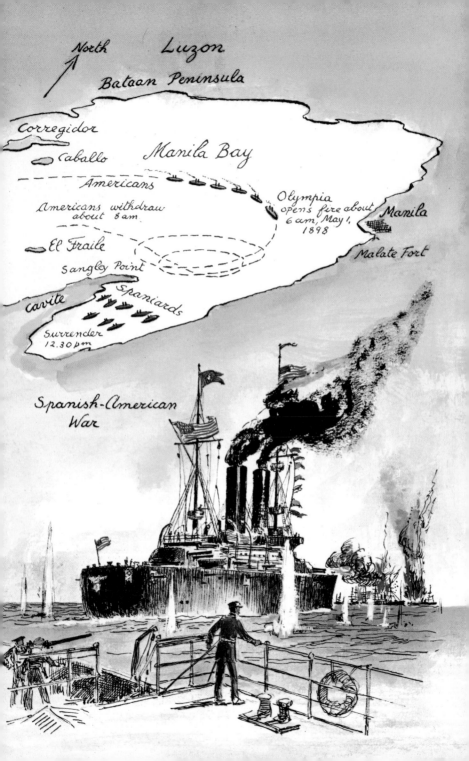

North
Luzon
Bataan Peninsula
Corregidor
Caballo
Manila Bay
Americans
Americans withdraw
about 8 am
Olympia
opens fire about
6 am, May 1,
1898
Manila
El Fraile
Sangley Point
Malate Fort
Cavite
Spaniards
Surrender
12.30 pm

Spanish-American
War